INTRODUCTION TO CHRISTIAN ETHICS

INTRODUCTION TO CHRISTIAN ETHICS

Friedrich Schleiermacher

TRANSLATED BY JOHN C. SHELLEY

■

Abingdon Press
Nashville

INTRODUCTION TO CHRISTIAN ETHICS

Translation from the German language of Friedrich Schleiermacher, CHRISTLICHE SITTENLEHRE EINLEITUNG (Wintersemester 1826/27) with the approval of the Publishing House Verlag W. Kohlhammer, Stuttgart, West Germany. © 1983 by Verlag W. Kohlhammer GmbH, Stuttgart.

English translation copyright © 1989 by Abingdon Press

This book is printed on acid-free paper.

Library of Congress Cataloging-in-Publication Data

Schleiermacher, Friedrich, 1768–1834.
  [Christliche Sittenlehre Einleitung. English]
  Introduction to Christian ethics / Friedrich Schleiermacher :
    p. cm.
  Translation of: Christliche Sittenlehre. Einleitung.
  ISBN 0-687-19500-4 (alk. paper)
  1. Christian ethics. I. Shelley, John, 1944– . II. Title.
  BJ1253.S3213   1989
241—dc20   89-7031
                                                CIP

Scripture quotations, unless otherwise noted, are from the Revised Standard Version of the Bible, copyright 1946, 1952, 1971 by the Division of Christian Education of the National Council of Churches of Christ in the USA. Used by permission.

Those noted KJV are from the King James Version of the Bible.

MANUFACTURED BY THE PARTHENON PRESS AT
NASHVILLE, TENNESSEE, UNITED STATES OF AMERICA

ACKNOWLEDGMENTS

My first words of appreciation go to Peter Hodgson and Jack Forstman, my teachers at Vanderbilt University, who stimulated my interest in Schleiermacher and encouraged my efforts at translation. It was in Forstman's seminar on Schleiermacher in 1971 that I presented a paper on "The Christian Ethics" and prepared a rough translation of about sixty pages from the Jonas Edition of *The Christian Ethics,* which was distributed to the members of the seminar. I returned to the project briefly in 1979 with the help of a summer stipend from the National Endowment for the Humanities, but then the project was shelved again until 1988, when Davis Perkins, formerly of Abingdon Press, inquired about my translating the new Peiter Edition. Davis has been a most patient and understanding editor and has contributed immensely to the translation itself. I am also grateful to several members of the Furman University Community. John Crabtree, Vice President for Academic Affairs and Dean, arranged for a reduction in teaching load during the 1988 fall term. Albert Blackwell, my colleague in the Religion Department, who understands Schleiermacher far better than I, offered numerous illuminating suggestions. Jane Chew and Norman Whisnant of the German Department provided essential assistance in deciphering some of Schleiermacher's ponderous prose. Connie Quillen also contributed substantially with her competent secretarial assistance.

Finally, a special word of thanks to my wife, Anne, and to my two sons, Mark and David. All three take an interest in my work and offer their own forms of encouragement, but they also help me to keep these scholarly endeavors in proper perspective.

John C. Shelley
Furman University
March 1, 1989

CONTENTS

Translator's Notes.. 11

Chapter One: TRANSLATOR'S INTRODUCTION........... 15

The Intellectual Context of *The Christian Ethics*......... 15

The Christian Ethics Within Schleiermacher's System.. 21

The Organization of *The Christian Ethics*.................... 26

The Jonas and Peiter Editions of
The Christian Ethics... 28

Schleiermacher and Contemporary Christian
Ethics.. 30

Notes... 31

Chapter Two: INTRODUCTION
TO CHRISTIAN ETHICS.. 33

The Close Relationship Between
Theology and Ethics.. 33

The Unique Character
of the Christian Community.................................... 35

The Restriction of Ethics to a
Present (Peaceful) Time.. 38

The Restriction of Ethics to the
Distinctive Spirit of the Protestant Church................ 39

The Relationship
to Rationalistic Theology
and to the Rational Ethics of Duty............................ 41

The Consciousness of God as Principle of Action..... 44

Thought and Act
as Similar Primordial Expressions
of an Even More Primordial Tendency...................... 46

The Necessity of the Strictly "Dogmatic" Form......... 48

The Use of the Moral in Holy Scripture................... 49

The Relationship
of What Is "Pleasing to God"
to the Fact of Redemption.. 50

The Ethical Consequences of a Superhuman
Representation of the Person of Christ...................... 52

The Congruity of
"Moral" and "Dogmatic" Errors.................................. 54

The Ethically Relevant Principles
of the Reformation.. 57

The Benefits of the Conflict
Over the Proper Exegesis of Scripture...................... 58

The Replacement of the Imperative
by the Descriptive Form.. 62

The Overcoming
of the Old Testament Economy
in "Adoption": The Spiritual Coming of Age............ 64

The Discernment
of a Straightforward Description................................ 67

Consideration of the History of Ethics...................... 69

The Purifying Power of Conflict................................. 70

The Distinction Between
Self-expressive and Efficacious Behavior....................71

The Impulse to Action
Modified by Pleasure or Pain.......................................73

Joy in Christ and Communion with the World.........75

Relationship of the Particular to the
Universal Formula...77

The Significance of "Dogmatic"
Differences for Ethics...80

The Engagement of Piety
with Actual Political-Social Relationships....................82

Expansions and Advancements...................................83

Identification with the Whole
and Opposing Points of View......................................85

Eliminating the Debates
Over the Principle of Ethics
and the Capacity for Moral Behavior.........................87

The Difference Between the Church Militant
and the Church Triumphant..89

The Two Focal Points of Christian Ethics.................90

The Antithesis Between Protestant
and Roman Catholic Churches....................................92

Positive and Negative Morality..................................93

The Significance
of the Doctrine of the Church
for the Organization of Ethics.....................................94

The Priority of the Christian Life
Over Christian Ethics...96

The Conflict of Duties:
Conceptual and Temporal...97

The Efficacious Elements
in Self-expressive Behavior,
and Vice Versa.. 99

The Subordinate Dichotomy:
Disseminating and Corrective Behavior.................... 101

The Exhaustiveness
of the Classification in the Types
of Behavior Derived from the Church
Militant and the Church Triumphant...................... 103

The Resolution of Conflict.. 103

The Beginning of Morality
in the Perception of Contradiction
Between Old and New.. 107

TRANSLATOR'S NOTES

The writings of Schleiermacher confront the modern translator with a host of almost insuperable problems. The syntax is incredibly complex, often befuddling even native German speakers, and the various nuances of key terms rarely coincide exactly with their English equivalents. The most obvious difficulty in the present work concerns *Glaubenslehre* and *Sittenlehre*, which I have translated, respectively, as "theology" and "ethics." It is true that compound constructions like "faith-instruction" and "moral-instruction" would be technically more accurate and would better preserve the parallel character of the two disciplines, but current usage of "theology" and "ethics" seems pointed enough to identify clearly the two disciplines that Schleiermacher has in mind, and yet broad enough and fluid enough to allow Schleiermacher's own distinctive understanding to emerge. Also, these terms certainly enhance the readability of the text.

The words *Wissenschaft* and *Wissenschaftlich* are typically rendered "science" and "scientific," respectively, but in modern English these terms have become identified almost exclusively with the natural sciences, which suggest objective empirical observation and mathematical modeling. Hence I have opted here for constructions like "conceptually rigorous" to suggest that for Schleiermacher theology and ethics are "scientific," not because of commitments to objective empirical observation and mathematical modeling, but because they are nonspeculative and demand intellectual coherence, critical reflection, and logical ordering. The term *Geist* ("Spirit" or "spirit") raises a peculiar problem: When should "spirit" be capitalized? Schleiermacher uses the word to refer both to the Holy Spirit and to the "common spirit," or character that defines a specific historical community. The problem arises in connection with Christianity when Schleiermacher affirms that the "spirit" of a particular church is, in some sense, an empirical manifestation of the Holy Spirit. Although both Protestantism and Catholicism are manifestations of the Spirit, their "common spirits" are fundamentally different. I have capitalized the word only when it seems to refer to the Holy Spirit in the abstract, apart from its historical manifestations in particular communities.*

For obvious reasons I have used "Protestant" to translate *evangelische*. *Handeln, Handlung,* and *Tatigkeit* have been fairly consistently translated, respectively, as "behavior," "action," and "activity." With some hesitation I have rendered *Lust* and *Unlust* as "pleasure" and "pain," although clearly these are not to be understood in a utilitarian sense. The various types of behavior described by Schleiermacher—*darstellende* ("self-expressive"), *wirksamen* ("efficacious"), *correctiv* ("corrective"), and *verbreitend* ("disseminating")—utilize ordinary terms. My first inclination was to translate all four terms with participles, but I finally

---

*See Friedrich Schleiermacher, *The Christian Faith,* trans. H. R. Mackintosh and J. S. Stewart from the Second German Edition (Edinburgh: T. & T. Clark, 1928), p. 535: "After what has been said, the expression 'Holy Spirit' must be understood to mean the vital unity of the Christian fellowship as a moral personality; and this, since, everything strictly legal has already been excluded, we might denote by the phrase, its *common spirit*."

decided to use common adjectives, except in the case of *verbreitend,* where "disseminating" seemed better than "diffusive," "propagative," or "expansive." The important thing is that Schleiermacher imbues these terms with his own distinctive meanings.

CHAPTER ONE

TRANSLATOR'S INTRODUCTION

THE INTELLECTUAL CONTEXT OF *THE CHRISTIAN ETHICS*

In his famous speeches to "the cultured despisers of religion,"[1] Friedrich Schleiermacher declared that the essence of religion is neither theology nor ethics. Such a bold challenge to prevailing notions of religion demanded justification, and Schleiermacher felt obligated to explain the connection between religion and dogmatics, on the one hand, and religion and morality on the other. The first task was fulfilled in *The Christian Faith*[2] where Schleiermacher pioneered a radically new understanding of the nature and ground of Christian theology. The second task was never finished, as Schleiermacher was unable to realize his dream of publishing a comparable companion volume on *The Christian Ethics*. That Schleiermacher was indeed interested in the subject is indicated by the fact that he lectured on Christian ethics twelve times between 1806 and 1831. The literary remains of those lectures—a few handwritten manuscripts from Schleiermacher himself and handwritten lecture notes from a dozen or so students—give us some idea of his thoughts on the subject.

In preparing and revising his lectures on "Christian

Ethics," Schleiermacher was responding, directly and indirectly, to a variety of intellectual and religious currents. The Renaissance and Reformation had challenged in radical ways the synthesis of faith and reason that had undergirded the moral vision of Thomas Aquinas and other medieval thinkers. A wedge had been driven between faith and reason, and this sparked a hostile debate over the fundamental ground of morality. The questions were not new, but they did have renewed urgency. What is the ultimate source of morality? Whence come the criteria for "right" and "wrong," "good" and "bad"? Does morality rest solely on divine commands? Can reason provide the criteria for defining "right" and "good"? Is morality simply a matter of "might makes right"? Is morality purely an individual matter, deriving from the desires and fears of each person? Does morality stem from the goals and purposes embodied in one's community? Schleiermacher inherited an incredibly complex situation as he sought to remain a Protestant theologian and at the same time work within the critical spirit of the Enlightenment.

The Reformation Tradition

While Calvin clearly had a much greater appreciation for reason than did Luther, both reformers followed William of Occam in forsaking appeals to natural law and refusing to offer any rational justification for morality. Luther's hostility toward Aristotle in *The Babylonian Captivity of the Church* and his contention that "reason is a whore" are indicative of this tack. Morality is based strictly on the commands of God and neither requires nor permits any external justification. In fact, attempts to offer rational vindication were a form of "works righteousness" that violated the principle of justification by faith alone. An action was "good" or "right" simply because God commanded it, not because of the intrinsic character of the action itself or because of some vision of human nature or social good based on empirical observation or deductive logic.

In Luther and Calvin this objective, transcendent norm of morality was tempered and qualified by the subjective experience of grace and forgiveness. Justification by faith meant the surrender of all attempts at self-justification. Two of its corollaries, "freedom from the law" and "the universal priesthood of the believer," removed from Christian experience the emphasis on obedience to law. A new disposition, not law, became the focus of morality in the Christian life. As Luther put it: "Good works do not make a good man; but a good man does good works."[3] Believers acted neither out of fear nor out of the need to prove themselves worthy of grace, but out of love and gratitude. To be sure, the believer remained at once saved and sinner, but the focus of morality had decisively shifted from the objective commands of God or the church to the inner transformation of the person.

This did not mean, however, that the will of God could be discerned directly from human experience, even from the experience of justification by faith. Morality, like doctrine, was linked to the principle of *sola scriptura*, and Calvin compared the Bible to spectacles that enable us to see more clearly. But again the doctrine of the priesthood of all believers and respect for individual conscience qualified the objectivity of morality found in Scripture. However, Protestant Orthodoxy sharpened the notion that God's revelation is essentially verbal and that the Bible is to be understood as a direct verbal communication from God to human beings. Faith became identified less with an attitude of existential trust and more with intellectual assent to revealed dogma. Similarly, the command of God became explicitly identified with various biblical injunctions—for example, the Decalogue, Proverbs, the Sermon on the Mount, and the moral pronouncements of Paul and others. The individual was addressed directly by God through Scripture and proclamation and thereby confronted with the choice of whether to obey or disobey. Christian ethics, under this model, was little more than codifying, clarifying, and harmonizing the various biblical injunctions.

Schleiermacher apparently regarded the Protestant Orthodoxy of the early nineteenth century as a degenerate Protestantism, and he firmly rejected both its insistence that morality assumes the form of law and its claim that the content of Christian morality could be found in a list of biblical commandments. He based this rejection, however, on other Reformation principles, especially justification by faith and its corollaries in "freedom from the law" and the "universal priesthood of the believer." Thus in *The Christian Ethics,* after a very Lutheran interpretation of Paul (see below, pp. 62-64), he declares that Christian ethics is fundamentally a descriptive discipline. What he means is that Christian ethics, founded on the Pauline notion of "freedom from the law," rejects the imperative as the primary form of ethical propositions. Rather, Christian ethics is properly concerned with the indicative, that is, with describing the distinguishing characteristics of the Christian life. The description is normative, even though it does not explicitly command or prescribe. Schleiermacher continues to hold to the principle of *sola scriptura,* but for him the Bible is not a sourcebook for objectively revealed moral precepts. Rather it is a book that informs the Christian conscience and thus helps to shape the Christian's impulse to action. The individual whose conscience is informed by Scripture is finally his or her own judge in matters of morality.

The Enlightenment

If the Reformation located morality in the revelation of divine commands, the Enlightenment sought to ground morality in reason. Thus John Locke appealed to the self-evident truths of reason as the basis for his theory of human rights: the right to life, liberty, health, and property. At the beginning of the Enlightenment reason was viewed as supplementary to revelation, or vice versa, but gradually reason became the equal of revelation and finally replaced it altogether. Much of the appeal of a rational ethic was its claim to universality. Since reason was assumed to be the same in all persons, many were convinced that reason could provide the basis for a universal ethic that would unite all people. Religion divided people; it was hoped that a rational ethic could unite them. Thus reason itself became that which provided the criteria for right and wrong and the stimulus for moral action. In such a climate the whole notion of "Christian" ethics is called radically into question. What sense does it make to speak of "Christian" ethics when reason posits that its own claims are universally binding? If reason is indeed the source of norms and the impulse to action, then the qualifier— "Christian"—is surely superfluous.

The towering figure in this move to join morality to human reason was Immanuel Kant (1724–1804). Kant, who in a paradoxical way both fulfilled and annulled the movement, is a particularly helpful foil for understanding Schleiermacher's Christian ethics. Kant's theory of knowledge, developed most fully in *The Critique of Pure Reason* (1781), limited knowledge, properly speaking, to the phenomenal world, that is, the natural or sensible world that we come to know through our senses. The categories of knowledge—for example, the notions of cause and effect, and space and time—through which we interpret the natural world are actually structures of the mind that organize sense experience, thereby transforming mere sensation into real knowledge. Since the phenomenal world adhered strictly to various laws, Kant designated it as a realm of necessity, a world without freedom. The implications of this epistemology for traditional religious thought are radical indeed. For one thing, it suggests that there can be no knowledge, properly speaking, of supersensible reality, and that undermines in a radical way the metaphysical claims of traditional Christian theology. Reason and revelation were widely assumed to give knowledge of God, including knowledge of God's will, as in Protestant Orthodoxy.

But human experience is not limited to knowledge of the natural, phenomenal world. There is also the *noumenal* world, the world within, the world of immediate experience. It was here in this world of immediate experience that Kant located the source of morality. He called it "practical reason," thus distinguishing it from "pure reason," which gives knowledge of the natural world. It is practical reason that enables the human being to grasp the moral law within. The moral law, for Kant, is strictly "deontological"—that is, an action is defined as "right" or "wrong" solely on the basis of the character of the action itself, without regard for the consequences. Kant adamantly insisted, for example, that telling the truth is always right, and lying is always wrong, regardless of the consequences of each.

With regard to the moral agent, however, the character of the action itself was not sufficient to establish the morality of the agent. The motive for acting was also crucial to Kant. Basically, there were two kinds of motives, corresponding to two kinds of imperatives: hypothetical and categorical. A hypothetical imperative was teleological or consequentialist, taking the form of: "If you desire this, then do this!" Hypothetical imperatives were derived from one's inclinations, our leaning in a certain direction because of biological, social, or psychological factors. These inclinations were determined, shaped, and conditioned by the phenomenal world, therefore bearing its deterministic character.

The categorical imperative, on the other hand, is grounded solely in the notion of duty. One acts simply on the basis of duty, without thought of consequence. To do the right deed simply because one is inclined that way and therefore "enjoys" it is not a moral act. An act is truly moral only if one acts out of duty. If I tell the truth, for example, primarily because I know the truth will bring me special recognition, then I have not acted morally, even though I did the "right" thing.

Thus Kant pictured the human being as suspended between the polarities of inclination and duty. Inclination belongs to the phenomenal world, the realm of necessity, and as it follows desire it often pulls in a direction opposed to the categorical imperative. But Kant assumed—indeed required—a notion of freedom in which the agent is always capable of choosing duty over inclination. Thus freedom becomes a postulate of practical reason, as do God and immortality.

Schleiermacher concurred with Kant's critique of pure reason that confined knowledge, properly speaking, to the phenomenal world, but he disagreed radically with Kant's description of the moral agent. Reflecting both his Reformation heritage and a critical appropriation of Pietism and Romanticism, Schleiermacher resisted Kant's essentially dualistic account of human nature, which posited an absolute line between reason and nature, between the noumenal and the phenomenal worlds. Schleiermacher sought to develop a more dialectical model of the self, where reason and nature always exist together and where each conditions the other. Thus inclinations do play a major role in our moral choices. It follows that my moral responsibility includes not only specific choices that I make in the moment, but also the development of a pattern of life that shapes my inclinations in such a way that I become "more inclined" to do the right thing. Thus the moral life is conceived as a process which should move in the direction of bringing my inclinations more and more under the control of reason, or to use the language of the New Testament, to bring the flesh into harmony with the Spirit.

THE CHRISTIAN ETHICS WITHIN SCHLEIERMACHER'S SYSTEM

Philosophical Ethics and Christian Ethics

The Christian Ethics occupies a clearly defined place within Schleiermacher's grand architectonic schema. Schleiermacher accepted the fairly common distinction between the natural and historical "sciences" and believed that all knowledge belongs under one category or the other. The theological disciplines, whose basic purpose is the guidance of the church, obviously belong in the historical category, along with empirical disciplines like psychology and political science. The foundation for these historical sciences is what Schleiermacher calls "philosophical ethics." For him ethics is "the science of the principles of history"[4] and thus more closely akin to what we today call the philosophy of culture, the philosophy of history, or even sociology.[5] The basic purpose of philosophical ethics is to provide categories of understanding, elements of a conceptual framework, that will enable the pursuit of more specific studies. Schleiermacher states: "Without constant reference to ethical principles, even the study of historical theology is reduced to a kind of haphazard calisthenics, and is bound to degenerate into a process of handing down meaningless information."[6]

Schleiermacher's Christian theology and Christian ethics are both historical disciplines that actually presuppose philosophical ethics, for it is the latter discipline that provides the basic categories of understanding that will be employed in the construction of the former. Thus the philosophical ethics are introduced in the very first chapter of *The Christian Faith*. In fact the first third of chapter 1 (about thirty pages in the English edition) is devoted to developing the conception of the church from "propositions borrowed from ethics."[7] It seems obvious that Schleiermacher's use of the term "ethics" is far removed from our popular association of ethics with rules and maxims that guide behavior.

More concretely, for Schleiermacher, "ethics" refers to the process through which nature gradually becomes the organ of reason. In other words, ethics is the process by which reason permeates nature and gives it shape or form. This process is most literally visible, say, in a work of sculpture or in the development of technology, whereby raw materials are given shape and/or organized in such a

22

way as to perform useful functions for human beings. But it is also evident in the continuing development of the great human communities—state, society, school, and church—that distinguish civilization from the primal conditions of the past. What is striking here is the breadth of Schleiermacher's ethical vision. Ethics is not one corner of life or simply the province of the individual. It quite literally encompasses all of finite reality.

This moral process, which Schleiermacher believed happens at all levels of nature, becomes conscious in human beings, so it is not surprising that a large portion of the philosophical ethics is devoted to a kind of phenomenology of human existence that delineates the essential structures of human life and the activities by which reason extends its dominion over the realm of nature. Schleiermacher's analysis is far too extensive for this short introduction, but two ideas are particularly helpful for understanding *The Christian Ethics*. First, Schleiermacher emphatically resisted the reductionistic tendencies of both idealism and materialism, insisting that human life consists precisely in the dialectical unity of nature and reason (in Kant's terms, the phenomenal and the noumenal). Against Kant, Schleiermacher insisted that each pole of this dialectic conditioned, and in turn was conditioned by, the other. Thus human life assumes the form of a struggle to bring nature into harmony with reason. But this is neither a Manichaean dualism in which nature and reason are eternally at odds, nor a Pelagian naivete that assumes too easily the dominion of reason. Schleiermacher's moral subject was not as radically free as Kant's noumenal self, which was not affected by the phenomenal self. By virtue of genetic inheritance, experience, and so on, one leaned or was inclined in a particular direction, and these inclinations figured prominently in moral choices, as they contributed to the "impulses" that provided the basis for human action. This description of human nature figures prominently in *The Christian Ethics* in the way Schleiermacher describes the

Christian life as a process of gradually bringing the flesh into harmony with the Spirit. It is just this tension that underlies the basic forms of efficacious behavior that give the basic structure to Christian ethics.

A second theme from the philosophical ethics that helps to illumine *The Christian Ethics* is the social conception of the self. The dialectic of reason and nature is crossed by a second dialectic, namely that between the individual and the community. A part of immediate self-awareness is the reciprocity between self and world, and the self is constituted not in radical individuality but in its social relationships. The individual can have an impact on the community, but the individual is in turn acted upon and shaped by the community. Thus human inclinations are powerfully shaped by one's associations with other human beings, especially in intentional communities like the church. Hence it is not surprising that the church, as the community of faith, plays a prominent, indeed foundational role in Schleiermacher's Christian ethics. As a descriptive discipline Christian ethics focuses on the community, not on the individual.

There are obvious tensions between philosophical ethics and Christian ethics that Schleiermacher has not adequately resolved. It is a fundamental claim of Schleiermacher that reason is one, which means that he allows for no essential contradiction between either the scope or the content of philosophical and theological ethics. He does insist on a difference of form, but his identification of philosophical ethics with the process by which nature is gradually brought into harmony with reason raises some very acute questions: Are not Christian ethics entirely superfluous? How can both philosophical and Christian ethics be necessary? Are they not indeed contradictory?

Theology and Ethics (Glaubenslehre and Sittenlehre)

As conceived by Schleiermacher, theology and ethics are closely related parallel disciplines. Strictly speaking, they are independent, with neither being derived from the other. This relationship is at least partially intimated by Schleiermacher's carefully chosen terms: *Glaubenslehre* (literally, "faith instruction" or "doctrine of faith") and *Sittenlehre* ("ethical instruction" or "teachings on morals"). Theology and ethics belong to "dogmatics" in the broader sense[8] and together comprise the church's teachings on faith and morals.

For Schleiermacher, of course, the essence of religion is neither theology (as in Protestant Orthodoxy) nor ethics (as in the Enlightenment, especially Kant). It is not essentially a way of knowing nor a way of acting. Rather the essence of religion is the "feeling of absolute dependence," which is modified in a variety of ways in its actual expression. Thus the "feeling of absolute dependence" underlies both Judaism and Christianity but it is shaped differently in these respective communities. Schleiermacher characterizes the distinguishing feature of the Christian modification as "the consciousness of sin and redemption in union with Jesus Christ." As a member of a religious community, therefore, one is shaped by its distinctive "spirit" or its peculiar modification of the feeling of absolute dependence.

For Schleiermacher this feeling of absolute dependence as modified in its concrete expression in the Christian Church becomes an impulse to thought (*Gedanke*) and action (*Handlung*). When the impulse gives rise to thought and thus comes to rest in a complex of ideas ("doctrine" or "dogma" in the narrower sense), that is Christian theology. When the impulse gives rise to action and stimulates a particular pattern of behavior, that is Christian ethics. Though closely related, both spring directly from the religious affections, neither being dependent upon the other. Thus ethics is not applied theology (as in much neo-Orthodoxy), and theology is not reflection on praxis (as in liberation theology).

Theology and ethics are both descriptive disciplines. That is, they describe the constellation of ideas (theology) or behaviors (ethics) that arise within the Christian community of a particular epoch. This description, however, is not strictly empirical, for it cannot be carried out by an objective observer standing outside the community who merely surveys attitudes about various moral issues. The description is more phenomenological and can be appropriately undertaken only by one who participates fully in the life of that community.

THE ORGANIZATION OF *THE CHRISTIAN ETHICS*

Schleiermacher's principle of organization of Christian ethics is based upon the types of behavior or activity that derive from the Christian consciousness. One may posit either two or three major divisions, depending upon whether "efficacious" (*wirksamen*) behavior is regarded as one type or whether each of its two subdivisions is treated as a major category. A twofold classification results from the dichotomy between "self-expressive" (*darstellende*) behavior and efficacious behavior. The major difference is that efficacious behavior specifically intends to produce an effect in the sense of bringing about change in oneself or in the world, while self-expressive behavior is just that—simply a desire to express oneself, to communicate with another, with no intention of producing change in oneself or in the world. A threefold classification results when efficacious behavior is further divided into "corrective" (*correctiv*) behavior and "disseminating" (*verbreitend*) behavior (see diagram). All this is considerably clearer in the Jonas edition of *The Christian Ethics,* where the ideas are more fully developed and the discussion much less abstract.[9]

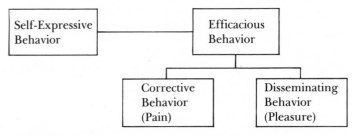

Diagram showing the Relationship of the Kinds of Behavior in Schleiermacher's Christian Ethics

Schleiermacher's twofold division of efficacious behavior is based on the claim that the intention to produce change in oneself or in the world can spring from two different impulses in the Christian consciousness. There are the impulses that derive from pleasure (*Lust*) and those that stem from pain (*Unlust*). For Schleiermacher the terms "pleasure" and "pain" refer to specific states of the Christian consciousness and have nothing to do with the utilitarian tradition fathered by Schleiermacher's contemporary, Jeremy Bentham (1748–1832). Schleiermacher conceives of the Christian life in terms of a continuum between the beginnings of one's desire for communion with God and the culmination of that desire in absolute blessedness. In other words, following Luther's dictum that the believer is at once saved and sinner, the Christian life in the real world is lived in the tension between sin and grace, between flesh and Spirit. Pain is experienced in those moments when one's communion with God is suppressed and one's dominant impulses to action are determined by one's lower nature. When those embued with a Christian consciousness selfishly hoard their possessions or when they lack the moral courage to take a stand for justice, they experience pain in the form of guilt and shame and in the ensuing struggle to regain one's moral bearing. The impulse that springs from this is what Schleiermacher calls corrective behavior because it seeks to correct or restore the proper relationship between one's higher and lower natures. Such action takes the form of punishment or discipline. The point is not that one's instincts or uniquely personal desires should be destroyed but that these should come to submit willingly to the impulses of the Spirit. According to Jonas' arrangement, Schleiermacher's discussion of raising children, criminal justice, and the ethics of warfare are all placed under the heading of corrective behavior.[10]

The experience of religious pleasure or joy resides in the consciousness of power that brings one's physical instincts and uniquely personal longings under the dominion of the Spirit. The religious impulse that springs from this is what Schleiermacher calls disseminating behavior because it seeks to extend the rule of the Spirit over oneself, over the church, and over the world at large. The specific form assumed by this behavior is education, both general education and specific training in moral and religious concerns. Thus here Schleiermacher addresses such topics as the nature of education, the role of the church in the educational process, and various issues relating to church-state matters.[11] Schleiermacher's concerns clearly have an eye toward social justice, and it is no accident that Walter Rauschenbusch hailed Schleiermacher as one of the "prophets" of social Christianity.[12]

Self-expressive behavior appears apart from the religious consciousness in play and art. There the point is not to change anything but simply to establish and maintain the moment of expression and communication. Within the religious consciousness this kind of behavior is found predominantly in worship. Worship is both corrective and disseminating, both within the community as a whole and within each individual, to be sure, but in genuine worship these elements are minimal compared to the impulse of self-expression.[13]

THE JONAS AND PEITER EDITIONS
OF *THE CHRISTIAN ETHICS*

For almost a century and a half the major access to Schleiermacher's work on Christian ethics has been the volume compiled and edited by Ludwig Jonas and published in 1843, nine years after Schleiermacher's death. Jonas had been a student of Schleiermacher at Berlin, having been especially captivated by the lectures on Christian ethics in the summer of 1817: "No lectures of Schleiermacher made a more powerful impression on me than those in the summer of 1817 on Christian ethics."[14] Two years later Jonas prepared a "detailed summary" of the lectures under Schleiermacher's supervision. Thus when Schleiermacher was unable to prepare the lectures for publication himself, he entrusted the task to Jonas. Jonas had access to four of Schleiermacher's handwritten manuscripts, but none was very extensive and each came from a different period in Schleiermacher's career (1809, 1822/23, 1828, 1831). Thus he had to rely heavily on students' notes. He decided to make the lectures of 1822–1823 the basis of the work, partly because he did have a partial manuscript of Schleiermacher from that term. From these materials Jonas published *Die Christliche Sitte,* a mammoth volume of over 700 pages.

The more recent edition of Hermann Peiter, from which this translation is taken, is based on the lectures of 1826/27. Peiter cites a letter written by Schleiermacher to Martin Leberecht de Wette in 1825, in which Schleiermacher says: "The thing I want most to do when I somehow find some spare time is to get to the Christian ethics as a parallel piece to the dogmatics. With my present reading they are becoming more polished, more complete, and more coherent than they were before. But nothing of this is getting put down on paper."[15] Hence Peiter argues that Schleiermacher himself judged the lectures of 1822/23 to be less than ready for publication, and that prompted his decision to publish an edition based on the lectures of 1826/27.

The Peiter text is a compilation from the notebooks of three students from that term, and it is limited to Schleiermacher's introductory lectures. The text can be a bit jarring at times, especially when the reader encounters references to Schleiermacher in the third person, but this reflects the nature of the materials at Peiter's disposal. In the German edition, Peiter has provided an elaborate text-critical apparatus that gives variant readings from the notebooks in footnotes. He has also provided copious references to parallel passages in Schleiermacher's other works, including references to Schleiermacher's handwritten notes utilized by Jonas. For the sake of facilitating a general appreciation of Schleiermacher's understanding of Christian ethics, neither of these helps has been included here. We have adapted Peiter's outline for a table of contents and headings in the text.

SCHLEIERMACHER AND CONTEMPORARY CHRISTIAN ETHICS

Schleiermacher has drawn woefully little attention from contemporary Christian ethicists. The new *Westminster Dictionary of Christian Ethics*, for example, contains only five incidental references to Schleiermacher, while Kant and Hegel each gets an entire article and numerous citations throughout the volume.[16] This situation is certainly understandable in light of the relative inaccessability of Schleiermacher's writings on ethics, but it is most unfortunate because Schleiermacher wrestles in a creative way with fundamental questions about the task of Christian ethics, the nature of moral agency, the relationship of Christian ethics to philosophical ethics. Some of his most prominent themes anticipate contemporary currents in Christian ethics. The challenge to Kant, for example, the role that community plays in shaping character, and the significance of character for moral decisions are strikingly similar to themes in the thought of Stanley Hauerwas.[17] Schleiermacher's respect for scriptural norms reflects the renewed

30

interest in Scripture and ethics.[18] The claim that ethics is a descriptive discipline, by which Schleiermacher means that the indicative is more fundamental for Christian ethics than the imperative, seems to have important connections with current interest in narrative ethics.[19] Thus it is hoped that the present volume will be a first step in bringing Schleiermacher into the contemporary conversations about Christian ethics.

NOTES

1. Friedrich Schleiermacher, *On Religion: Speeches to Its Cultured Despisers*, trans. John Oman (New York: Harper & Row, 1958).

2. Friedrich Schleiermacher, *The Christian Faith*, trans. H. R. MacKintosh and J. S. Stewart from the Second German Edition (Edinburgh: T. & T. Clark, 1928).

3. Martin Luther, *Christian Liberty*, trans. W. A. Lambert, revised by Harold J. Grimm (Philadelphia: Fortress Press, 1957), p. 24.

4. Friedrich Schleiermacher, *Brief Outline on the Study of Theology*, trans. Terrence N. Tice (Richmond: John Knox Press, 1966), sec. 29.

5. See Hans-Joachim Birkner, *Schleiermachers Christliche Sittenlehre* (Berlin: Alfred Toepelmann, 1964), p. 37. As with the Christian ethics, Schleiermacher's philosophical ethics have been reconstructed from his handwritten manuscripts and his students' notes. The standard text is *Philosophische Ethik*, in *Schleiermachers Werke im Auswahl*, edited by Otto Braun and Johannes Bauer, 2nd ed., vol. 2 (Leipzig: Felix Miner, 1927–1928). In preparing this section of the "Translator's Introduction," I have relied most heavily on three secondary sources: (1) the aforementioned work by Birkner; (2) Albert L. Blackwell, *Schleiermacher's Early Philosophy of Life: Determinism, Freedom, and Phantasy*, Harvard Theological Studies, 33 (Chico, Calif.: Scholars Press, 1982); and (3) James O. Duke, "The Christian and the Ethical in Schleiermacher's Christian Ethics," 1985. (photocopied). Blackwell's book, although it focuses on the earlier writings of Schleiermacher, is a particularly good introduction to Schleiermacher's ethical thought.

6. Schleiermacher, *Brief Outline*, sec. 29.

7. Schleiermacher, *The Christian Faith*, pp. 3-31.

8. Schleiermacher, *Brief Outline*, sec. 194-231.

9. Friedrich Schleiermacher, *Die christliche Sitte*, edited by Ludwig Jonas, 2nd ed. (Berlin: G. Reimer, 1884.)

10. *Ibid.*, pp. 97-290.

11. *Ibid.*, pp. 291-501.

12. See Walter Rauschenbusch, *A Theology for the Social Gospel*, (Nashville: Abingdon Press, 1945), p. 27.

13. Schleiermacher, *Die christliche Sitte*, pp. 502-705.

14. See Ludwig Jonas, "Vorwort des Herausgebers," in Schleiermacher, *Die christliche Sitte*, p. v.

15. Cited by Hermann Peiter, "Einleitung des Herausgebers," in *Schleiermacher: Christliche Sittenlehre. Einleitung*, edited by Hermann Peiter (Stuttgart: Verlag W. Kohlhammer, 1983), p. xxvi.

16. *The Westminister Dictionary of Christian Ethics*, edited by James F. Childress and John Macquarrie (Philadelphia: The Westminster Press, 1986). One of the few sustained treatments of Schleiermacher by a contemporary Christian ethicist is James Gustafson, *Christ and the Moral Life* (Chicago: The University of Chicago Press, 1968), pp. 83-98.

17. See, for example, Stanley Hauerwas, *Character and the Christian Life: A Study in Theological Ethics* (San Antonio: Trinity University Press, 1975); and *The Peaceable Kingdom: A Primer in Christian Ethics* (Notre Dame, Indiana: University of Notre Dame Press, 1983).

18. See Bruce C. Birch and Larry L. Rasmussen, *Bible and Ethics in the Christian Life* (Minneapolis: Augsburg Publishing House, 1989); Thomas W. Ogletree, *The Use of the Bible in Christian Ethics: A Constructive Essay* (Philadelphia: Fortress Press, 1983); and William C. Spohn, *What Are They Saying About Scripture and Ethics?* (New York: Paulist Press, 1984).

19. See James McClendon, *Ethics: Systematic Theology, vol. 1* (Nashville: Abingdon Press, 1987); and Hauerwas, *The Peaceable Kingdom*.

CHAPTER TWO

INTRODUCTION
TO CHRISTIAN ETHICS

THE CLOSE RELATIONSHIP BETWEEN
THEOLOGY AND ETHICS

Christian ethics [*Sittenlehre*] and Christian theology [*Glaubenslehre*] are very closely related, although this is not indicated by the terms themselves. As one looks at the history of theology, it is clear that the fashioning of Christian ethics as a separate discipline can be regarded as something recent. Abelard was the first to make that attempt, but he failed to find a way to do it. Not until sometime after the Reformation were the two disciplines separated and approached differently, as they are today. Danaeus and Calixtus accomplished this first.* The subject itself cannot have been altered by this separation, and the things that have been separated are intimately connected. Still less can one say that the individual propositions with moral content have, as a result of this division, received a new nature or that they have been specifically compiled for today. Even now the individual moral propositions have the same nature as the individual propositions of Christian theology. Thus it is inevitable that Schleiermacher would

---

*The reference is to Lambertus Danaeus, *Ethices christianae libri tres* (1577), and Georgius Calixtus, *Epitomes theologiae moralis pars prima* (1634).

treat this discipline differently than has been customary. It is unmistakable that ever since these disciplines were divided, Christian ethics has more and more been formed in such a way that, taken as a whole, it is regarded differently and that its individual propositions are grounded in a different way and attached to values different from dogmatic propositions.

Since the separation of the two disciplines, Christian — ethics has become more and more associated with rational ethics, and that has radically altered its whole relationship to dogmatics. However, this distorts the subject immensely, and as we consider the purpose of all theological disciplines, it is again necessary to abandon this approach throughout, because here Christian ethics is drawn entirely from the analogy of the other discipline and its own purposes are obscured. If we claim that faith should stick to the rule of Scripture or to analogy with what actually takes place in the church, and now insist that Christian ethics should be based upon reason, the latter is treated as a general human concern and not in terms of what takes place in the church. Therefore the first principle is this: The division between ethics and theology must never be allowed to destroy the analogy between the two. This principle is the foundation from which we must start. (See Schleiermacher, *Brief Outline on the Study of Theology** and *The Christian Faith*.)**

The whole schematic of the discipline of theology, as presented in Schleiermacher's *Brief Outline on the Study of Theology,* surely departs from the traditional approach, but the divergence is more semantic than substantive. Irrespective of what is known there as philosophical theology, the difference lies in the fact that the traditional approach sets historical and systematic theology side by side as two entirely different entities. Schleiermacher, however, totally eschews

---

Brief Outline of the Study of Theology, translated by Terrence N. Tice (Richmond: John Knox Press, 1966).
**The Christian Faith,* translated from the Second German Edition by H. R. Mackintosh and J. S. Stewart (Edinburgh: T. & T. Clark, 1928).

the expression "systematic theology." It is in terms of this expression that Christian theology and ethics have traditionally been understood.

Under the general heading of historical theology, a distinction is made between the knowledge of historical development in the Christian church and the knowledge of the actual present situation of the church. It is under this latter rubic that Christian theology and ethics are placed, a fact that certainly appears as a paradox but is not. It is true that this seems to suggest a very limited view of the matter, as if Christian theology and ethics were nothing more than the knowledge of that which currently passes for doctrine in the Christian church. In spite of all that, no explanation is necessary to show that what has traditionally been called systematic theology could be established here. However, the apparent paradox is that both theology and ethics should be explained as the connected understanding of that which takes place in the church. One could say: The knowledge of what is valid in the church can be acquired in a wholly external way, and in that case Christian theology and ethics would be nothing more than such a wholly external tradition, a collection of those particular propositions that have been expounded as doctrines of a congregation. These would contain nothing conceptually rigorous, nothing useful to theologians, and nothing appropriate to the purposes of theology. If theology and ethics expound only what holds true for a particular time, then there is no direction, no support, and everything goes on just as it always has. That is certainly not what Schleiermacher had in mind.

THE UNIQUE CHARACTER OF THE CHRISTIAN COMMUNITY

The Christian church is a community which is a living whole and understood in living development, but in such a way that each individual is affected by the whole and understands himself only in terms of the whole. For the Christian, in regard to the Christian community, it must be totally immaterial whether he says, "I take that for the truth," or whether he says, "That is the real sense and the real meaning of the Church." If this is not so, then he has left the genuine, living relationship to the Christian church. If one views the Christian church as a community and wants to say that the same holds true for every community, Schleiermacher will not agree, for he considers the Christian community to be totally unique. If we consider a state in a healthy situation, we can also say in a certain sense, the state is a whole understood in living development, but such that each individual feels moved by the whole. However, the state can be conceived only in a fixed form. When this change occurred, how did it come about? Has the state remained the same, or has it become something different? That is only a semantic conflict and can be disregarded. The form of the state belongs very much to the essence of the state, and this is what has changed. Could that have happened while all individuals were understood in terms of the whole? By no means! The individuals who changed this are therefore superior to it. In the Christian church changes have also taken place, but none which allows comparison with changes in the state and none that have destroyed the continuity such that one would not know whether the church was the same. There every improvement is joined to an earlier time, already past, even if occasionally it is disregarded by the present situation. Therefore, nobody in the Christian church can claim something as true for himself without at the same time claiming it as valid in the church; and if he has the majority against him, he will appeal to an earlier situation. If we now posit such a total complex of doctrine, can this perchance accommodate what should someday again be regarded as true? That is not possible, and can be made valid only by the prominence of the individual, because it is established polemically. The Reformers were in the situation of having to revalidate the earlier truth of the church. Did they do that through systems? No, but through the lifting up of the individuals and through comparison with what was once valid. If someone wants to revalidate an earlier complex of doctrine, then he must first win his point with individual propositions. The principles of the Reformation were already alive earlier in many individual people. But would a single witness to the truth of the Reformation have been capable of setting up a purely Protestant dogmatic? No, because he would always be returned to the polemical form. Consider, for example, from a theological perspective, Melanchthon's well-known dogmatic work *Loci*. Is that, strictly speaking, a Protestant doctrine of faith? No one can affirm that, because there is there no uniform wholeness and no precise connection. It is primarily the bridge from the polemic of an individual member to the authentic systematic connection.

By virtue of their conceptual rigor, both disciplines have a certain similarity with metaphysics and rational ethics. But has someone proved in every case that a system of metaphysics or ethics is a manifestation of that which is valid at a certain time in the philosophical world? No. The distinction is this: Neither the philosophical world nor the general moral world is a closed community like the Christian church. Yet everyone also stands in a closed community of language, and no one can bring something to light which is not already intimated there. *Anfang?*

Those who have the most complete consciousness of that which really moves in the Christian church can always piece together the views prevailing in the church about the right and the good and communicate those views. This is a much more intimate and more conceptually rigorous process, that is, the schematic of the whole is not found in a merely external way such that one must first have all the pieces; rather, one must ask: What are the necessary functions in which the authentic Christian spirit expresses itself in life? A much more internal process. For one who makes such a statement, it must not be something external, like so and so is valid in the church; rather, he bears in himself the character of the time which he portrays; otherwise, a heathen could also write a Christian ethics, in which case the inner conviction would be missing. Only a purely empirical description is consistent with the fact that it is given without conviction. The conviction, which is fully conscious, brings forth the conceptually rigorous form. Since Christian ethics can contain nothing other than the description of the same form of behavior that develops naturally from the Christian principle, it is always only in and for the Christian church.

THE RESTRICTION OF ETHICS TO A PRESENT (PEACEFUL) TIME

Considering the matter from this higher standpoint, how is it justified that Christian ethics can be given this portrayal only for a particular time? It follows from what has been said that Christian ethics can occur only in a time viewed in the whole as peaceful, where what is affirmed forms the great standard, obscures the conflict, and appears as something disconnected. We see how the whole movement of time is actually divided in this way. Also, according to the way such movement occurs, we see how the modification of the Christian life can develop in significant moments. If we could immerse ourselves totally in the life of an earlier time, then we could give internally and with conceptual rigor a description of that which was affirmed as right and good in that time. No longer, however. Such descriptions are surely very rare and difficult and always remain a critical operation.

Christian ethics, therefore, can be produced only in relation to a prevailing peaceful time in the Christian church. We cannot be certain whether everything that we now establish as right and good will be so regarded in the future any more than we now accept everything that had validity in other times. In our sphere every such movement is always a deeper immersion into the Christian principle itself, not an abandonment of that principle, nor an attack upon it. For that reason we must conclude that those who are called to explicate a Christian ethics, even those who have been deeply moved by the Christian spirit of their time and therefore were in a position to penetrate with clear consciousness its connection to life, cannot say that such and such will be valid for all future times, else they must have already anticipated the movement. To wish to pinpoint this is incompatible with the circumstances under which the Christian ethics takes place. It is good to be aware, however, that we still have nothing perfect and that something more nearly perfect will surely follow. Strictly speaking, the teacher of rational ethics should also have this consciousness. But it is a different matter in a closed community where one has progressively practical knowledge that the community develops in definite stages. If one had considered searching in a conceptually rigorous manner from the beginning, one would already have a number of ethics and theologies.

THE RESTRICTION OF ETHICS TO THE DISTINCTIVE SPIRIT OF THE PROTESTANT CHURCH

If, therefore, in Christian ethics we are restricted to a particular time, we also cannot dismiss another restriction. In the present time there cannot be, even for this time, a universal Christian ethics, because the Christian church is a divided phenomenon. If we focus on the one part of the Christian church where theology always progresses—that is, on the Western church—a division would actually be false, provided it consisted only of a division such as between the Church of England and the German Protestant Church. Though constitutionally separate, they stand united against the Roman Catholic Church, from which they are essentially separated in the manifestation of Christian faith and life.

Christian ethics, as it is manifested at present, can only be Protestant or Catholic and by no means both together. Just as we cannot set up a Christian theology that is neither Protestant nor Catholic, the same holds true for Christian ethics. The principle on which our entire Christian ethics must be constructed is the Christian spirit, but only as it appears in the Protestant church and not in its alternative modification. This point must be examined in more detail. The usual explanation of this relationship is that the Christian spirit is manifest in purer form in the Protestant church than in the Roman Catholic Church, where either it is contaminated by foreign elements or it does not permeate the people to the same degree. According to Schleiermacher's expressions, however, the meaning is quite different. The point is not that the Christian spirit is given more absolutely in the Protestant church and with deletions and additions in the Catholic. Rather, when Schleiermacher says that the Christian spirit in this modification is the basis for Christian ethics, it means that Schleiermacher accounts for the divergence of the Catholic Church, not in terms of abuse, but in terms of a distinctive form. The proof for this cannot be undertaken here. If the total difference between the two churches is that commonly assumed, then a Protestant ethics could substitute for the Catholic ethics of the same era. All we would have to do is juxtapose our more complete ethic to that which is less complete, and similarly, where something foreign has crept into the Roman Catholic Church, place that beside the purer. From this perspective, we can have nothing to do with the other view, namely, that the Roman Catholic Church is simply a distinctive form of the Christian spirit and not merely distorted by deformed structures or false practices. Such a view is not able to accomplish what it should. According to Schleiermacher's view, a Catholic ethics is indeed a totally different type of ethics from the Protestant. A Catholic ethics would be taken precisely in all its parts to be different from the Protestant. Thus instructions and parallels from Catholic ethics serve only as illustrations.

THE RELATIONSHIP TO RATIONALISTIC THEOLOGY AND TO THE RATIONAL ETHICS OF DUTY

As a rule, if we have only a preliminary notion of how Christian ethics realizes its organizations as a whole, then we must construct for ourselves a concept of the character and essential content of the individual propositions. On this point Schleiermacher appeals to the Introduction of his *The Christian Faith*.

The propositions of Christian theology and ethics are in no way purely intellectual constructions. Rather they are reflections upon the Christian consciousness apprehended in a specific activity: They never express a universal truth; in order for them to be true for a particular individual, the person must first be a Christian. The Christian consciousness, viewed on the one hand in its immediate originality and on the other in its individuality, has been called *feeling*. In that case, the word denotes the primordial consciousness in its specific individuality. The particular propositions of Christian ethics, therefore, are nothing but expressions of the content of particular functions of the Christian consciousness. Here we can best answer the question regarding the relationship between Christian ethics and rational ethics. In the *Brief Outline on the Study of Theology*, Schleiermacher said that Christian theology is related to rational theology as Christian ethics is to rational ethics of duty. If we ask, What is rational theology? we do not answer in terms of whether there is or is not such a thing. Rather we set it up as a problem and ask, What must it be? What do we focus on in rational theology? We focus on the knowledge of God generated entirely from reason. This kind of knowledge is out of place in Christian theology and at most is relevant only as a proposition or corollary. This is because what has universal rational significance must also be valid for all human beings. Christian theology, however, is true only for Christians. In both cases the subject is the same, but

41

the task of rational theology is to produce the consciousness of God purely from universal human reason. This is also the relationship between Christian ethics and the philosophical ethics of duty. Why should the propositions of Christian ethics be considered in relation to philosophical ethics of duty and not to philosophical ethics of virtue? In both spheres this is a matter of widespread confusion, for the ethics of duty and the ethics of virtue are jumbled up. The concept of virtue refers to something internal, an inner disposition that comes to light through action and, as such, something permanent, unchanging, always at hand. Duty has to do with particular deeds; therefore, in comparison with virtue, it concerns something external. Duty is the necessity of acting in a certain way and manner. It is appropriate when discourse focuses on problems of a particular moment. The propositions of Christian ethics, like those of theology, are only expressions of the Christian consciousness observed in its particular manifestations. The particular manifestations of what is moral are always actions, and the Christian consciousness viewed in this individuality is the Christian conscience or the Christian moral feeling. It is to this that we must give attention. The propositions of Christian ethics, therefore, will be expressions of this determination of the Christian moral feeling.

It follows from this that the concept of duty will be dominant in ethics, but more about that later. The comparison of Christian theology with philosophical theology and Christian ethics with philosophical ethics of duty presupposes an identity of subject and method and, since we do not equate the two, also a difference. The question is whether or not identity and difference permeate both subject and method.

The subject of rational theology and Christian theology is God. The method of each is different, the former being a construction, the latter having its origins in the specifically Christian consciousness. The identity with respect to the subject is not perfect. What is said about God in rational

theology is not identical with the assertions of Christian theology. Rather what natural theology can affirm about God partially presupposes Christian theology and partially pushes it aside. Rational theology can go no further than to establish the form of the relationship between God and humankind in universal terms. Christian theology begins there. What is historical in its essential individuality cannot be represented in philosophy as something necessary. What is the situation in ethics regarding the identity of the subject? We have already clarified the difference in method. Christian ethics is only for Christians, and it can say only that the action to which the Christian principle drives human beings is such and such.

If Christian ethics is indeed limited solely to that which proceeds from the Christian spirit within the Christian church, the question is how, at the same time, it can encompass the whole of human life, which does not consist entirely of the relationship of the individual to the Christian church. If one refers back to the saying of Christ that "My Kingdom is not of this world," one could conclude that all actions relating to this world have nothing to do with Christian ethics. If we said that in some relations we must determine our actions from Christian ethics and in others from philosophical ethics, the possibility of conflict is already assumed. If we want to resolve the matter in another way and say the action of the Christian, even in the state, should always be governed by the rule of Christian ethic and that it must extend itself to cover that, then this possibility of conflict is abolished, and we have a right to say: The subject entirely the same. However, this appears to reopen the door all the abuse that has originated from the fact that the Christian church has claimed authority in worldly matters, and opposition between the Catholic and Protestant cannot de against it. Christian ethics should also guide the dominion worldly things, but only in a spiritual sense (because statesman could never act contrary to Christian e Christian ethics should establish its own decision principles over everything that can appear in the life of

43

beings, but the Christian church should use nothing other than the authority of the Word; and the multiple abuses have originated only when the decisions have been colored by worldly considerations.

In *Brief Outline on the Study of Theology* Schleiermacher states: A lot passes for rational theology that is really nothing more than elements of Christian theology, just as many things pass for rational ethics of duty that are nothing more than elements of Christian ethics. These are connected as follows: There are systems of ethics that want to be valid for philosophy but which, in the final analysis, are based throughout upon the moral feeling. This is especially true of the English moralists, whom the French and Germans have since followed. It is not a philosophical construction but rather a transfer of the distinctive form of Christian ethics to the philosophical sphere and thereby inadmissible. Philosophical ethics of duty should have universal validity for all, and yet the moral sentiment of Europeans differs from that of New Zealanders. No one in the Christian world can separate his moral feeling, which he wants to derive purely from human reason, from his Christian feeling; therefore, there enters into such systems so much that is also the content of purely Christian feeling. In relation to rational theology and Christian theology, the matter does not fit together in this way. There the issue is as follows: In the sphere of rational theology no one with consciousness can go back to the original Christian consciousness, and even then much enters into rational theology that would never have been able to be spoken according to purely rational construction without the fact of the Christian religion.

THE CONSCIOUSNESS OF GOD AS PRINCIPLE OF ACTION

Now a further word about the separation of the two disciplines insofar as it is something incidental. The

distinctive nature of the propositions of Christian theology is that they contain expressions of the Christian consciousness to the extent that the highest reality is set forth in them. The propositions of Christian ethics are expressions of the Christian consciousness as it expresses itself as moral feeling. Those are not different explanations. One can easily imagine a conceptually rigorous grouping of a complex of propositions of one or the other. If we returned to the time when theology and ethics were not yet separated, that explanation would seem unsuitable, and it might be concluded that such union should never have happened. However, since we said the separation of the two disciplines is nothing essential, but only incidental, the implication clearly is that the propositions of one discipline must be analogous and homogeneous with those of the other. Still a unity must be found here. It is this: When it is said that Christian ethics contains expressions about the Christian moral feeling, that does not mean that the consciousness of God should thereby have been excluded; on the contrary, it is the character of the Christian moral feeling that the principle of behavior should be nothing else but the consciousness of God. As far as Christian theology is concerned, it has not been said that the Christian consciousness has not always included the principles of Christian behavior. For example, if we adhere to the propositions of the Christian consciousness that affirm the attributes of God, then we must certainly proceed from the fact that these are always understandable only in relation to one another. However, if we construct only one combination—for example, between divine omnipotence and divine love—then we must say that this combination leads to trust in God, and that is already a principle of behavior. It must be possible in the Christian sphere to accomplish in form what Spinoza accomplished in the philosophical sphere, namely, to treat everything as ethics. Theology could appear in ethics, albeit incompletely, just as ethics has appeared in theology.

Thus, in the most precise accord, we must imagine that Christian consciousness as that in which the highest reality is set forth and Christian consciousness as that which includes the source of actions are entirely one and the same. But now we will see that an even greater kinship occurs among theoretical propositions and among practical propositions when they are delineated with conceptual rigor.

THOUGHT AND ACT AS SIMILAR PRIMORDIAL EXPRESSIONS OF AN EVEN MORE PRIMORDIAL TENDENCY

What has been said can always leave the impression that the two disciplines stand in a hierarchical relationship, with dogmatics claiming the dominant place. There is also something to be said for historical appearance, since it was dogmatics that first developed intellectually. The moral has likewise become autonomous, but the dogmatic was always presupposed. But this impression is detrimental to the subject and therefore not directly valid. The drawback is this: We know, as it presently pertains to our dogmatic theology, how many contrary methods are present in our church. If in the case of Christian ethics one must appeal to dogmatics, then morality would become entangled in these dogmatic disputes. However, we must contend that there are also differences in morality that are independent of those to which dogmatics currently succumbs. The same morals can even be linked to different dogmatic systems. (The above cited examples of trust, omnipotence, and love always give this impression.) The point is not that these dogmas as such must be assumed in order to have trust in God. Christian faith is indeed assumed, but only in the form of the primordial consciousness, not dogmatic develop-ment. It is assumed that there was a Christian life before there was Christian ethics. One can certainly say that the apostles have given Christians directions from which the Christian life has arisen. That cannot be refuted. However, in that case the Christian life already existed in the apostles themselves. How then does the Christian life originate? It presupposes Christian faith, but only in the sense that Christian faith is prior to Christian theology. The primordial Christian consciousness is precisely Christian faith, and that has two aspects existing side by side, one aimed toward the thought, the other toward the act.

We can demonstrate this identity of the Christian consciousness in a very general way if we hold the Christian consciousness before us. The question now is how a thought and an action originate. In both cases human beings are assumed to be alive and in union with the surrounding world, which acts upon them. Any specific moment of life has always been composed of these two elements, but that which overflows into thought is exactly the same as that which overflows into the act. The primordial consciousness, strictly speaking, is indifferent in its bearing on the two. Sensation is not possible without life, just as it is not without influence on something. Either of the two—that is, the thought or the action and deed—can arise from this influence and from life. Either is then prepared for the situation, begun by the influence, to seize it or to break free. By degrees, the same is true with the higher spheres of life which we illustrate here. That life which includes the consciousness of God is presupposed as an impulse or tendency, not as a thought. If one imagines an influence in any relationship, the direct result could just as well be a thought as an act. It becomes a thought when I reduce what is expressed to its effective ground; it becomes a deed when I find in it a summons to act in accordance with the divine will. Consider the first encounter of Andrew and John with Jesus. The influence of the divine was there first, and from that arose a thought and a deed. The thought was that we have found the Messiah; the deed was that they began to communicate with him. The primordial, from which both things arose, was the impression of the divinity of the redeemer. Thought and deed sprang equally from that, neither being dependent on the other. Both stand

47

equidistant from the primordial. If, therefore, we want to bring a more nearly perfect clarity to our particular propositions and trace them back to the primordial source, we must not return to dogmatic propositions, but to that which underlies these particular dogmatic propositions.

THE NECESSITY OF THE STRICTLY "DOGMATIC" FORM

But we will have no more precise way of getting back to the Christian consciousness than choosing the more strictly dogmatic form. This project, proceeding in this way, is already a radical departure from the customary approach. The way and method subsist in the Christian ethical description of the Christian life, but the Christian life is not the pure manifestation of the Christian consciousness. It has always contained the imperfect. If we must represent the Christian consciousness, since we have to proceed from it, then we must understand that we intend the Christian consciousness in its primordial condition. In that case, it is often possible that we express it through the idea. For that reason, we want to choose the dogmatic form in which there is no deviation.

In assimilating Christian ethics to rational ethics, the customary approach has its merits. If we look carefully at Scripture, we find there, according to form and substance, no distinction between theoretical and practical propositions. Both are expounded in the same manner and in similar form. Therefore we must also persist in that. Whoever wants to reduce Christian theology to philosophy may and can also reduce Christian ethics to philosophy. Whoever does the one and not the other is inconsistent. Schleiermacher wants nothing of either. The idea of the Christian church must lead and govern the whole enterprise. Our entire theological development in the recent past has embraced the notion that this idea is of very little importance. This has its roots in the antithesis between Protestantism and Catholicism, but there is no necessity in what one observes from books of doctrine.

THE USE OF THE MORAL IN HOLY SCRIPTURE

Having asserted that Christian ethics should be nothing but the manifestation of the Christian life, how do we establish that what we take up in Christian ethics is actually the pure expression of the Christian principle? Here we can give only the following answer: We have to establish this from its agreement with Scripture. This answer has its ground in what we as Protestant Christians believe about the standard authority of Scripture. In practice we find here a significant distinction between the respective methods of Christian ethics and theology. The same theologians who use a number of biblical texts in their dogmatic works use very few appeals to Scripture in their discussions of morality. Why is that? Is Scripture more sparing in moral than in theological concerns? That is not the case. Certainly the social relationships of that time were entirely different from what they are presently. The vital mistakes that had to be resisted no longer occur to us, and the same is true in connection with those things that gave value to other regulations. Not due to scarcity but in the inapplicability to the present situation— therein lies the issue. Here the *ignara ratio theologica* [ignorance of theological principles] meets us halfway. If we cannot make direct use of the specific regulations, we do have the general principles that we can employ in our situation and which we can then verify with Scripture passages. The specific regulations are to be made applicable for us by way of analogy. Therefore we do not need to pass over into the philosophical sphere, which will always govern Christian theology and ethics in form but never in substance. From

49

where, however, do we originally derive the substance? The intellectually rigorous method requires that substance originate conjointly with form and that both be developed from the same thing. Tracing its origins to Scripture gives the method its final confirmation. That is the way that we must distinguish our approach from rational ethics. That to which we appeal fundamentally is the pure Christian principle of life, which we find manifested in the Christian life itself. Having found this principle, we will be able to go to work entirely analytically. In this way it is only the rigor of form for which we have presupposed the rule of the philosophical method. We do not have to appeal directly to anything speculative and rational.

THE RELATIONSHIP OF WHAT IS "PLEASING TO GOD" TO THE FACT OF REDEMPTION

Now, however, we must first solve a preliminary problem, one raised by the foregoing statement that we can realize nothing other than Protestant Christian ethics. Thus even here, we must return to what was established anew by the Reformation as a Christian principle of life, to what we look upon as "the individual" of the Protestant Christian consciousness. Again, however, this is something common to both ethics and theology, involving no dependence of one discipline on the other. If we chose to adhere solely to what is common to all churches, we would in fact obtain only a very indefinite result. We must make sure, however, that we are capable of declaring the difference in the case of each individual proposition such that the consciousness of that is constantly with us.

Is there anything that can be considered the common ground of that which separates Protestant and Catholic morality? We will have to assume in advance a kinship between that which is the basis of separation in the sphere of dogmatics and in the sphere of morality. However, it is not yet certain that it is identical such that there must be an identical expression for dogmatics and morality. To attempt a solution now, we must return to what is common. If we do not wish to attempt too much here and again accept everything that belongs to the task of constructing the concept of what is authentically Christian, we can stop with this: The common element of all Christian doctrine is that the fact of redemption is acknowledged through Christ, and without this there is no Christian doctrine. The question is: What kind of effect does this have generally on Christian ethics, and how is this doctrine derived? Here we must go back to the still more general religious character of doctrine where it must be agreed that ethics is religious when it manifests and sanctions the activity as pleasing to God and so constructs it. But how should the fundamental fact of redemption through Christ be viewed in this respect? It is easy to show that it can take place in a twofold way. First, one says: The recognition of what is pleasing to God is independent of the fact of redemption through Christ, but in this fact Christianity has given assistance, which is not found outside of Christianity, for realizing the God-pleasing action. Does this fundamental belief of the Christian have an effect on the construction of ethics? No, because nothing is incumbent upon ethics in and for itself except to construct the whole range of human activity that satisfies a certain idea of the right and good. If recognition of the divine will has always existed prior to redemption, then no change can take place in the construction of ethics. At most it would be of influence in asceticism. Here we can return again to the attempt to reduce Christian ethics to philosophical ethics. Beginning with that presupposition, one should abandon the attempt to construct Christian ethics and simply add the individual propositions of dogmatics as postscripts. The question is whether another presupposition is possible. By all means, if we put the matter as follows: The idea of "pleasing to God" has itself emerged in another way through the fact of the divine revelation in the person of Christ, and adhering to this revelation of God in Christ was also a manifestation of the idea of "pleasing to God." In that case it is clear that there must be a Christian ethics. What exactly is this that has continually emerged in the Christian church as the Christian consciousness? If we begin with Christ himself, he lays the most certain claim to the fact that he has knowledge of God that can be communicated only through him, and that he sets forth a knowledge of God's will that did not exist before him.

THE ETHICAL CONSEQUENCES OF A SUPERHUMAN REPRESENTATION OF THE PERSON OF CHRIST

This is indeed clear, but those who proceed from the other presupposition offer another explanation: Christ was right because his knowledge of God was at that time not yet available. He spoke to his people, among whom there could not yet be the knowledge of what is pleasing to God; neither could it have been known by the Gentiles. Many have said: Christian ethics needs only to be assimilated to what is already available (Stoicism). Christ has revealed what is of God and the divine will, and without him that could not have become known until later. Thus the same thing is said, but now one adds an appendix: After we have considered how much Christ's teachings about God concur with human reason, it is natural to jettison the historical element and build solely upon human reason. Then it would be time to abandon Christian ethics and to explain what appears there as pure rational instruction. Now the question becomes: Is there another explanation of those words of Christ, and can one decide between the two? As long as reason has not attained this self-standing knowledge, it is clear that the moral teachings of Christ must be perceived as belonging

52

exclusively to him. Suppose, however, that after reason has attained this self-understanding, Christian ethics expounds this unequivocally as rational instruction. This happens because the intelligence is very reticent to relinquish its customary form, and there may be a certain wisdom in leading the soul to retain the form even now in practice. But it is clear that another interpretation is possible. Once it has been conceded that the moral prescriptions of Christ were available before him among neither the Jews nor the Gentiles, and that they have been made valid only in connection with Christianity, then one can assert correctly: Human reason would not have attained that by itself, and if it were to attain that in the present, that is to be ascribed only to the influence which Christ has had on it. This all depends upon the conception that one has of the person of Christ. If one has a purely natural conception, one must say: Christ can bring forth nothing except what human reason would also have discovered at a later time. However, if one says that with the person of Christ and through Christ something real has entered human nature, that something has appeared that was not previously there and that even now can come forth only insofar as the union with Christ persists, then one must concede that human reason does not yet have that on its own. Therefore the existence of a special Christian ethics stands or falls with the superhuman conception of the person of Christ. From a purely naturalistic view of Christianity, it is always contradictory to pursue a distinctly Christian ethics, and it is always consistent to turn it into the pure instruction of reason.

Christian ethics does indeed have connections to the person of Christ, but it also has another connection to the Christian church viewed as community. It will be truly valid only in and for the Christian church, and it will not solve the problem of behavior in a way that is universally binding. Rather, it will only show how it is treated in the Christian church in accordance with its spirit. It is, therefore, the ethics of a particular community. This is a separate point,

53

but the connection with what has been said is very easy to see. If reason reaches the point where it can develop this on its own, it would be inconsistent to expound ethics under the Christian form; but it would also be inconsistent to adhere to a human community like the Christian church. Christian faith involves the attempt to hold on to the Christian church. The transposition of Christian ethics into rational ethics is connected solely to the attempt to dissolve the Christian community and vice versa. Christian ethics is grounded therefore in the fact of revelation, but it is valid only for the community of the church.

THE CONGRUITY OF "MORAL" AND "DOGMATIC" ERRORS

At this point we can now engage the question of how things stand regarding the distinctiveness of Protestant Christian ethics, only we must first preface this with a historical observation. If we note the parallels between Christian theology and ethics, we find in the development of Christian theology that which is termed "heretical." How does the matter stand with reference to Christian ethics? Is there an analogy? And is there something special in this analogy? The first we must deny, because this matter can be treated only historically, and in that case we find no analogous condemnation from the Christian community instigated by deviations in Christian ethics. That certainly means that the Christian congregation, taken as a whole, has been patient towards deviations in morality. However, it may not be denied that only that which is not heretical in its dogmatic aspect should be an influence on morality.

In *The Christian Faith** Schleiermacher defines heresy so as to oppose the Ebionitic and Nazarean, the Manichaean, the Pelagian, and the Docetic heresies.

---

*See section entitled "The Impulse to Action Modified by Pleasure or Pain."

(1) Docetism—that is, all shades of the various views of the person of Christ that deny his humanity—has the effect of prohibiting the appeal to the example of Christ in ethics. Because the action is not human, it cannot be a model for human beings. Only that which is similar can be a model. The concept of Christian perfection does not require that there be someone else, but the argument will shift. If we recall that in the apostolic writings themselves Christ is set up as a model and that Christ sets up his own innermost disposition as the characteristic mark for all his followers, then it is properly concluded and consequently already demonstrated that docetism is contrary to Scripture. Nevertheless, this teaching has spread far and wide in a senseless manner even among the masses in our own church. One still finds quite often that the denial of Christ's humanity has been linked to the doctrine of the divinity of √ Christ. We see that there are still many things against which we have to be on guard. Certainly it should be easier for us to eliminate this teaching if we always return to Scripture.

(2) Ebionitism has a definite tendency to subordinate Christian ethics to the ethics of reason. If the specific distinction between Christ and all other human beings is abolished, it necessarily follows that Christ occupies a lower level, for the human spirit has clearly grown so much in general. Someone / can stand far above his generation, but finally there must come a time when even those who differ less from their contemporaries than he did from his, will supersede him. For that reason we must say that, generally speaking, wherever one finds the tendency to subsume Christian morality under the morality of reason, one also finds an unconscious inclination to Ebionitic and Nazarean views of the person of Christ, and yet the essential strength of the specific distinction between Christ and all human beings resists that. In this we stand on a more secure and more stable ground than the Roman Catholic Church, because throughout our system of doctrine and practice, this particular presentation of Christ is far more easily recognized than in the Roman Catholic Church.

(3) Manichaeanism is based on a natural dualism among human beings because it views evil as a reality in opposition to good and, as a matter of utmost consequence, as having equal primordiality and power. The battle between the principles of good and evil among human beings can be settled only according to the measure of strength of one or the other. Accordingly, there are human beings in whom the good cannot overcome evil. When carried out consistently, this view destroys all intentional influences on the morality of human beings. In that case some turn out to be persons who cannot conquer evil; therefore, for them everything is in vain, and yet others need nothing. This leads to passivity in the ethical sphere. Strictly speaking, this denies the whole point of a Christian ethics because there can be no talk of an outward Christian influence nor of an inward behavior. Then there can be talk only of a certain being of the Christian church but not of a certain action of the church. Here we must say: To the extent that Manichaeanism is lodged in theory and creeps into theology, in the same measure is the establishment of Christian ethics something unnecessary. The one displaces the other. In the Catholic Church the idea of the church is given such weight that, for this very reason, the theory of Manichaeanism, which opposes it, cannot prosper. It is a fact of history that so far as the idea of the church is manifest, the mere appearance of Manichaeanism provokes the most vehement reaction. Our history indicates that in the past the idea of the church has not stood out strongly enough. This is all the more reason why we must be on guard against the appearance of Manichaeanism.

(4) Pelagianism fosters a highly superficial morality, and both have always been bound together. On the one hand, the imperfection of human reason is acknowledged, but, on the other hand, not its absolute powerlessness. The divine grace is only a resource to make better use of the power inherent in reason. Thus it is always the case that only something imperfect can occur. Here again the deviation includes a principle that opposes the development of

Christian ethics and abolishes the distinction between theory and practice. If theory does not strive to become something absolute, it has been essentially abolished and there is no practice. Now one could ask: Has it perhaps been denied that ethics is valid only for a specific time? But that simply means that the understanding of Christian truth is always limited to a particular time. It cannot be denied that Pelagian tendencies and laxity in ethics have always run parallel. These deviations have been found under different forms at different eras in the Christian church, even during the era of schism in the Western church.

THE ETHICALLY RELEVANT PRINCIPLES OF THE REFORMATION

What is the characteristic principle of Protestant ethics? Clearly not the constant struggle against heresy, because we find that even in the Catholic Church. But now, by the formation of this contrast, has something been fixed whereby Protestant ethics can be precisely distinguished from the Catholic? As is now well known, the point around which the whole controversy revolved was the doctrine of justification by faith, which included the controversy over the worth or worthlessness of all external works. This is obviously a formative principle for the whole notion of ethics. A second major point was the abolition of the distinction between those-who-command and those-who-obey in the church and the establishment of an equality of all under Christ and the divine Word. Both are closely related to each other, and only from this can the influence on ethics be understood. It is most incorrect to say that the Catholic Church believes it possible to determine the worth of human beings through external works. To be sure, a few teach that; but for others such works would be expressions of the inner disposition, and that must come from obedience to the church. Were that not true, it would not be a church. The conflict, therefore, cannot be traced back to the disposition but to the church. In Protestantism we know nothing of obedience to the church, for this is the place of our common obedience to Christ himself. From this it follows automatically that everything that should be set down as prescription for the Christian life can be derived only from Christ and from Scripture. However, it also follows that all these representations are binding for each individual only insofar as one has the conviction that right is derived from Scripture. In the Catholic Church, always in the case of the laity, this is replaced by obedience to the church and the appeal to church authority. To be sure, the entire difference is not yet perfectly clear, but we pose a question: From where do the commandments of the Catholic Church come, and what is the norm for these commandments? That is clearly the issue. For the laity there is nothing but obedience to the church, and morality rests entirely in that. There is for the laity no possibility of ethics. They have the command of the church. But how does this command originate? Can it not originate in a right way or a wrong way? The task of Christian ethics is only to seek the answer to this question: What is right for the church to command and what not? What would be right for us would be that which each individual demands of himself. Given the situation in the Roman Catholic Church, where there is a sharp distinction between clergy and laity, Christian ethics must always be an arcane discipline. Otherwise, the authority of the clergy will be destroyed, or the laity will no longer need recourse to the clergy. The Roman Catholic Church can, if it wants to be consistent, reject the entire discipline.

THE BENEFITS OF THE CONFLICT OVER THE PROPER EXEGESIS OF SCRIPTURE

The Roman Catholic Church, in matters relating to theology and ethics and to church polity, does not go back to Scripture alone but places the tradition on a level equal to

Scripture. From where does the tradition come? The tradition is created by the clergy, and in order to render it equal to Scripture, it must be assumed that the tradition is inspired. The clergy, therefore, generate what they command in the name of the church with the actual help of inspiration. Here we see the difference between the Protestant and Catholic churches with reference to Christian ethics. Just like our theology, our ethics is a complex of teachings relating to the good that are drawn from Scripture. It is one and the same for all constituents of the church without any distinction between productivity and passivity, between giving commands and obeying. The commanding authority is always and only that of Scripture. If Scripture is the sole authority, we must conclude, according to our teaching, that what is explained differently in the Catholic Church is contrary to Scripture. We maintain that in ethics as well as in theology, and there the matter rests. It is well known that in our case theology always suffers from the uncertainty of interpretation, because proof texts are susceptible to a varied exegesis. We will proceed no further in the sphere of Christian theology except to say that we affirm the following: It will not be completely finished until there is a perfect exegesis of Scripture, that is, it will always be evolving.

How does this matter stand with Christian ethics? Essentially we have no reason to maintain that its relationship would be any different, but in its appearance it proves to be otherwise. It is not to be denied that in the Protestant church disputes over morality also arise. In disputes over moral prescriptions one does not usually appeal to Scripture, as in the case of theology, but remains more often in the rational sphere. If we examine the issue carefully, we must admit that the New Testament does not attend as much to moral discussion as to dogmatic, and thus *?* there is less material in this case to occasion differences in exegesis. However, if we turn to the individual expressions of Scripture, we indeed find such incoherence between those and the expressions of our own language that a different exegesis arises, and from those ethical representa-

59

tions a different ethical character develops. This, however, is more than simply a minor problem. If Christian ethics should reach its completion in this way, there will still be disputes with respect to exegesis that have not yet been advanced. Consider, for example, the interpretation of *makrothumia* [patience] and *hupomone* [endurance].

If we consider how the general cosmopolitan circumstances of the Christian church have changed drastically from what they were in the New Testament period, it seems self-evident that we can no longer make use of many prescriptions, and for many situations in our lives we find no prescription in Scripture. Contemporary non-Christians who live among Christian people stand in a totally inverse relationship from that of the first century. And as for the political relationships, there are absolutely no prescriptions. Hence it also happens that even in Christian lands theories have been established about the relationship of politics and morality that assume the former exists independently of the latter. Here, therefore, on the one hand, is the task of Christian ethics to refine its approach to Scripture and indeed more precisely than has been customary. On the other hand, the task is also to restore in some way what is missing for present relationships. How can this restoration be accomplished? We must here employ an interpretation like the judicial where laws from an earlier time must often be applied to situations arising in the present. The main point is that one correctly determine the circumstances either by right principles or by analogy with other circumstances addressed by prescriptions in Scripture.

The same process exists in theology as well. Can we actually depend so heavily on that principle that separates us from the Catholic Church, or will we not have recourse to something entirely different? The important thing is that the analogy between the two be correctly formulated. In Christian theology we make use of our doctrinal books; and if we can prove something from those, we often look upon scriptural proof as unnecessary, but without placing the doctrinal books on par with Scripture as the Roman Catholic Church does its tradition. However, our opinion is that the interpretation of Scripture that we acknowledge is the same as that underlying the commandments of the doctrinal books. But in general there is no way we can assume that. Therefore, it will always be a fetter for Protestant churches that someone can charge us with interpreting Scripture according to the scriptural interpretation of the doctrinal books. The doctrinal books, therefore, are evidence only to the extent that we can still accept their interpretation of Scripture. It is no different in Christian ethics. However, the fact that the doctrinal books do not give us appropriate substitutes for matters not addressed by Scripture does not result so much from their having been set in direct moral opposition to the Catholic Church. The opposition was strictly dogmatic.

Do we now have anything other than Holy Scripture? And may we appeal to anything other than Holy Scripture and the propositions that accord with exegesis? If we also admit that ethics is only a manifestation of what is valid in the Christian church, it appears that we can have a totally different ground of proof. What is truly valid in the practical sphere of a community is what we call custom [*Sitte*], and if we can further specify the customs according to the Protestant church, then that is acknowledged as the norm of good and right. However, that cannot be separated from scriptural evidence and set out independently, else it becomes tradition. In that case custom is also something traditional, and further, the custom could even arise from a misunderstanding. There are sufficient examples of that in the Protestant church. Therefore we shall always have to point out that something is custom in the church and to what extent it is custom. But we may not establish that by itself without appealing to Scripture. This reference back to custom in morality can have no other purpose than this: One decides in the individual moment whether Scripture agrees with the custom or not. To understand the diverse character of particular teachings is part of the task of ethics.

THE REPLACEMENT OF THE IMPERATIVE
BY THE DESCRIPTIVE FORM

Beginning from the distinction between the Protestant and Catholic churches, let us ask what form the particular propositions of our ethics should take. What first suggests itself is that they should have the form of commandment. Then again one could insist that another form would be more appropriate. Since not all commandments are stated explicitly in Scripture, this approach seems to lean toward Catholicism. In that case, who is the one giving commands? If propositions were always the pure words of Scripture, then one would know that Scripture is the one giving commands. But propositions are often developed from Scripture, and then the developer—namely, the theologian—appears as the one giving commands, and this must not happen. The more the church is ruled by the civil arm, the less each will be upheld. If something is commanded in relation to the Christian life, the Christian will then see that it proceeds more from the civil arm. Though we have no obligation to choose the giving of commands as the form for Christian ethics, it would still be good to do in order to breathe new life into the distinction between clergy and laity. In addition to the commandment, we find another form already in Scripture which alone is sufficient reason to prefer it to the other. This twofold form found in the New Testament consists of the already mentioned commandment (in the maxims of the apostolic letters and the teachings of Christ) and then the purely descriptive form, which we find in the most crucial passages—as, for example, in I Corinthians 13 where we find the description of *agape*, which still occupies a major place in morality. There nothing is commanded, but simply stated that it is such and such. The same is true in Galatians where the *karpoi tou pneumatos* [fruits of the Spirit] are described. From this passage [Gal. 5:16-24], in which Paul renounces the law, one could draw a further conclusion and assert that he meant not only the Mosaic Law—though surely that is the main point—but also the legal form in general. One must think of the moral law generally. How else can it cohere with Paul's statement that "You are not under the law"? One cannot think of the Mosaic law without thinking of the moral law of the Decalogue. In that case, what is the essence and the distinguishing feature of law? Law is given where it is presupposed that the content of the law would not be followed if the law were not given. The contrary is always presupposed. The same is true in politics. According to Paul, that statement can refer only to the form, not to the content, of the law, and then one sees clearly how this encompasses the whole of human life. Wherever the Spirit is and wherever human beings develop for themselves the fruit of the Spirit, there is no longer any connection with law. For such persons the law no longer exists. If we conceive the task of Christian ethics as assembling those propositions which are actually followed as a result of the operation of that Spirit, then we see how the form of law is unsuitable for this content. As Paul said: "You are not under the law." If now and again the imperative form creates the impression of a commandment-giving faction in the church, it seems most appropriate to renounce that form and adhere to the other. If now, based on Paul himself, it can be ascertained that he made use of the imperative form, we will discover that this is natural where he writes generally to *neophutous* [neophytes] in Christianity, for whom the Spirit does not yet have power over the whole of life. Surely this is continually the case in the Christian church, and there is none for whom the law is not necessary, at least at times, though it is purely ascetic for each individual. We conclude that the form of Christian ethics that most clearly expresses the spirit of Christianity is the antithesis to law. However, one is free to put oneself or another under the form of law where it is necessary.

Considering the usual practice, we find the commandment to be the dominant form, and so it is natural to ask how that could have originated, inasmuch as we consider it incorrect. On the one hand, this draws its main support from the relationship that one seeks to give to Christian and philosophical ethics. This has taken a different form in different times. During ancient times the descriptive form more often prevailed. Thus in Stoicism the archetype was the description of the wise custom, while in Aristotelian thought it was the description of virtue. However, in more recent moral philosophy the ethics of duty has generally predominated, and there the form of commandment emerges. If we want to investigate whence this has come, we will hardly know where to begin except with this: The development of universal ethics has, on the one hand, been joined to politics (where law rightly dominates). History offers still another clue: Philosophical ethics has developed, not from what exists in science, but more from what is found in the common public life. Through the medium of rational ethics it has returned, via the practice of Christianity, in the didactic form of academic theology. That practice, however, was catechetical, and thus that ethics was developed from the practice of pedagogy, where even the commandment has its natural place. Two very different things have to be considered here.

THE OVERCOMING OF THE OLD TESTAMENT ECONOMY IN "ADOPTION": THE SPIRITUAL COMING OF AGE

Since we base Christian ethics on Scripture, we must ask what Scripture is. Is it the New Testament alone? Or both testaments together? Or the New Testament as an appendix to the Old Testament? The more one concedes and assigns to the Old Testament, the more the command-giving form will dominate, because this is what carries weight in the Old Testament. However, Paul's cardinal passage in the Epistle to the Galatians should provide the ground to deny the Old Testament the right to determine the form. When Judaism was a theocracy, there was a confusion of politics and religion. The main form in which God was held in consciousness was political, for God was conceived as sovereign. The natural development of this general consciousness in the individual included the notion that the divine will appeared in the form of commandment. In Christianity this necessarily must be otherwise, not only because particularism is abandoned, but because the relationship is conceived differently from the very beginning. In Christianity the will of God does not come to us so much as it arises within us through the union in which Christ stands with God. Each individual is in the Christian church only to the extent that there exists between him and Christ a unity of will like that between Christ and God. The true essence of Christianity and the way in which redemption should be conceived in moral terms is this: The will of God arises within us through communion with Christ. Therefore a form that represents the will of God as something external can no longer be regarded as correct. Rather we must say that in the State itself the greater the unity between the individual and the whole, the less laws are necessary. The more we stress this characteristic Christian standpoint, the more the imperative form appears unsuitable. The form of pure statement, however, implies in each moment that something gains validity only by virtue of the Spirit ruling in the Christian church. On the other hand, it can still be said that in one passage Christ himself lays down his entire will for his disciples in the form of a commandment, *entole*: "A *kaine entole* [new commandment] I give to you" (John 13:34). But what is the content of the commandment? In a literal sense the form [of the commandment] cannot be applied at all to this content because the content is love. Love is a disposition, and a disposition can never be commanded. Therefore, that is either a figurative or an elliptical expression, or the content is to be understood indirectly. But, no, Christ wanted to set forth love as that by which he would recognize his disciples; therefore, *entole* is not to be taken literally. If one looks

65

carefully at customary usage it is clear that the expression is really elliptical: I give you a *kainon* [new]—instead of "all"—*entole*, to which all commandments should be applied. "One can be recognized as my disciple only if he bears this disposition." Thus it appears that this passage can directly support the relinquishment of the imperative form.

Another issue ensues. What is the Scripture on which we want to base Christian morality? It is the New Testament. It is certainly contrary to the whole practice of the Christian church and therefore inappropriate for Christian ethics to want to exclude the Old Testament. The issue, however, is this: When Paul says the law has been a *paidagogos* [pedagogue] which through *uiothesia* [adoption] receives its dismissal with the spiritual maturation of human beings in Christianity, he means the entire Old Testament period. The principle of all Christian ethics, upon which rests everything that is to be presented in Christian ethics, is none other than the *pneuma hagion* [Holy Spirit]. Paul himself said that the *pneuma hagion* had first come after God had sent his Son, therefore only after the New Testament period. This Spirit did not exist in the Old Testament. Apparently opposing this is another dogma of our church, namely, the *unitas ecclesiae* [unity of the church] from the beginning of the human race. However, this dogma is to be used with great qualification so as not to obscure what is essentially Christian. We certainly concede, though not absolutely, a genuine connection between the economies of the Old and New Testaments and therefore a historical unity between them. The whole Pauline perspective speaks for this. However, that is no reason for asserting that the divine Spirit in the Old Testament economy is the same as in that of the New Testament. Otherwise, the Spirit would not have been sent first by Christ. That Spirit appears in the Old Testament only in reference to the prophecies, and therefore it is only seed for the New Testament. What is not justified on the basis of the Old Testament, however, is the claim that the moral propositions standing in the Old

Testament must be set forth in Christian ethics. But this does not extend so far that one needs nothing as evidence from the Old Testament. (1) Whenever we have in the New Testament clear passages that include the substance of moral propositions in more stringent form, nothing is necessary from the Old Testament. But when we find in these New Testament passages something simultaneously rooted in the Old Testament, then this belongs to the explanation of the New Testament passage. (2) Should the substance of evidence be present in the New Testament only through quotations from the Old Testament, then this is the argument of the New Testament itself. Strictly speaking, therefore, we stay with the New Testament. (3) What is not cited in the New Testament, however, and is to be found only in the Old Testament is pernicious and may not be accepted. Otherwise the whole legalistic spirit can too easily enter.

THE DISCERNMENT OF A STRAIGHTFORWARD DESCRIPTION

The important thing now is to lay down a principle for organizing the whole. Generally speaking, the matter stands like this: What we want to describe should be nothing other than Christian morality rightly understood, and this description, properly ordered and encompassing the whole, is Christian ethics. Christian morality is the Christian spirit, which we regard as the principle of actions. These actions are expressions of the Christian spirit and therefore in harmony with it.

On the relationship between Christian morality and ethics, Schleiermacher assumes that the purpose of all theological disciplines is the proper guidance of the Christian church. But this suggests a contradiction regarding the form of Christian ethics. Because if Christian ethics is the description of Christian morality as it appears in the

Protestant Church, the question is this: Is our ethics the description of the Christian morality that presently exists in the Protestant church? Or is it, as description, something discerned, a morality that is yet to come? In the first instance, the purpose of Christian ethics as a theological discipline appears to be entirely lost, for one cannot change a thing by describing it. Should the second point, that Christian ethics transcends the present, be valid, then it would only appear to be pure description, for it would always imply at the same time: That is how it should be. That is the way the matter is manifested here.

However, if one observes this a bit more closely, it appears that it is not entirely accurate. It is certainly true that something does not improve immediately when one simply describes it as it is. But whenever perception is granted validity as a living power, and good and evil are described, the living power lying within perception is awakened when perception is communicated. The purpose of ethics, the guiding of souls, therefore, is not lost, but the description must be so conceived that it both accurately reveals mistakes and makes possible the perception of the difference. When the matter is framed in this way, the gift of discernment already lies within it because what is present in the sphere of ethics is simply incomplete insofar as falsity remains and the object has not yet been fully mastered. Everything truly moral in the Christian church has its ground in the Christian spirit. Wherein lies the ground of this falsity? In that which the Scripture calls the "flesh." However, this is also the object over which the Christian spirit should become master. Therefore, some part of human action still has its ground in the flesh, that is, the flesh is not yet subordinate to the Spirit. When the activity of the Spirit is described, there will emerge with that a description of how that activity will be shaped if it is developed further. That is precisely the element of discernment. In terms of the purpose of Christian ethics as a theological discipline—namely, the proper guidance of the church—we lose nothing if we stay with our previously indicated form. But can we be certain that the present imperfect situation of morality does not affect our ethical teaching itself? We cannot be certain, as we have already stated, because each Christian ethics is determined only for a particular present time. However, in order that everything be done—and it can only be done where the manifestation itself springs forth from the time—it is absolutely necessary to adjust our description so that, throughout, the antitheses in the sphere of Christian morality will be exposed, and we must constantly be prepared to examine how our description stands in relation to these antitheses. The problem is to identify these antitheses as much as possible for each epoch by a formula which, for the most part, excludes them. Then the standard by which the description is tested will be given at least in the description itself; and it can at least include the seeds of improvement, even if they are not represented right away.

CONSIDERATION OF THE HISTORY OF ETHICS

In Christian theology, since it has been separated from Christian ethics, two different approaches have been distinguished: the description and arrangement of Christian dogma and the description of Christian history. This division is in no way so general and so complete that both are not joined together in many dogmatic works. In Christian ethics this separation is not yet practical. Just as Christian morality is itself a historical life, the reflection on it—that is, ethics—also has its own history; and without this history it is not possible to fully understand its teachings. This is more striking in dogmatics because most doctrines are developed in conflict and bear these traces so clearly. In Christian ethics the matter is not yet so completely clear, but surely one must concede that the ethics of each epoch depends on the historical context. For the reflection on the inner disposition, in order to manifest it as instruction, is in and of

69

itself directed ambiguously toward the whole; but it would never happen like this in reality. If we observe, however, a change of epochs, it is precisely individual points that precede the change, and this lies precisely in history. Such points are Christian propositions which therefore depend on the historical context and cannot be understood without it. Here the historical is not yet so isolated that it can be treated as a different subject. Thus it becomes advisable to return to the historical context at such points where the formulation of the teaching especially demands it.

THE PURIFYING POWER OF CONFLICT

When we look especially at the character of our description of a Protestant ethics, we must still make a further distinction. If we go back to the beginnings of Christianity, we see that it described itself as a new life. Thus it was natural, even though the task was to fashion a new moral life from this new principle, that much opposed to the essence of Christianity was carried over into that life. The circumstances of the early church were such that it greatly facilitated the perception of contradiction. If the congregation consisted only of Jews, the contradiction could not be perceived so easily; but if the congregation consisted of Jews and Gentiles, contradictions could become more obvious. This applies to the genesis of the Protestant church. There is no such duplicity in the struggle of the Protestant church against the Catholic Church. The Protestant church had to take all its members from a prior community and therefore missed the purifying struggles. It is natural, therefore, that a lot of things were not changed for a long time before it was recognized that they were opposed to the spirit of the Protestant church. Hence we can in no way concede that elements of a Protestant ethics found in the earliest period of the Protestant church are the most perfect. Rather that statement is valid only for what was brought to consciousness in that time directly through conflict. However, what remained without contradiction cannot immediately be deemed the most pure. Therefore, we must describe as wrong much that was earlier validated as right. The same is true for what existed prior to the Reformation and also for what was taken over into Protestantism. If we consider what is genuine in the Protestant church, we must put ourselves on guard not to consider everything in terms of whether or not it requires modification, just as, on the other hand, we must confess that even during the Reformation other contradictions were raised against what was valid. These arose from a fanatical aberration and from errors that misjudged the distinguishing characteristics of Christian principles. From the beginning the Protestant church has struggled earnestly and continually to separate itself from both. Many things, however, have entered into Protestant practice and teaching that already have a positive relationship with those two sides. This historical element, which actually lies outside the Protestant church, is the second thing that we must always have at hand when making our description. These are the major points that, with respect to description, we must always have in focus.

THE DISTINCTION BETWEEN SELF-EXPRESSIVE AND EFFICACIOUS BEHAVIOR

The characteristic spirit of Christianity is a principle of action that should encompass the whole of life. Against this, however, an objection can be raised immediately. One can say that the distinguishing essence of Christianity exists not in action, but in rest [*Ruhe*]. That is also a part of our conception of God, and the community with God, therefore, would also be a community characterized by the divine rest. The activity of God

71

was the Creation, and since then the being of God has been manifested as rest. Similarly, the essence of Christian perfection in the future life has not been portrayed as an advance in activity. The highest human perfection is portrayed as rest in the contemplation of God and God's self. Therefore, activity would not be a product of the Christian spirit. Activity would be only a means to attain that rest and, strictly speaking, would be viewed only as a necessary evil. However, that will certainly not fit with what was said earlier, and we will have to see how these differences can be resolved. It is true that in other New Testament passages, apart from Revelation, the future life is represented as having no activity, only rest. The situation of the Christian who has reached perfection is what we call happiness [*Seligkeit*]. Inasmuch as complete satisfaction is then assumed and inasmuch as action arises from need, there can be no action when there is no need. Can there be an action that does not arise from need? One must distinguish between an action that is strictly internal and one that bears on external subjects. The first must always be present, else life itself would disappear. In the second case, one must ask by what means other than by some deficiency one will initiate action and cause something to change. One must also note that a deficiency does not correspond to happiness. It is already implicit in perfect happiness that no imperfection exists any longer, not only in human beings themselves, but also in what surrounds them. Then the impulse to action ceases. The question now is whether, in that case, every behavior directed outward also ceases. If there is no behavior other than what will produce change, then there is nothing else to be said. However, there is a behavior directed outward that proceeds essentially from internal activity and originates from it, but without intending that change should be the result. We find hints of this even in the description of the absolute happiness of Christians. For everywhere in these descriptions, Christians are conceived as part of the ongoing community since their situation is never spoken of in Scripture except as one of a community. Mere coexistence, however, is not a community, for to community belongs a circulation, a communication of life. There is absolutely no internal behavior of human beings that is not also, at the same time, an outward behavior, which, strictly speaking, is only a communication of what is internal. Only under this condition can a community persist. The situation of perfection should be a situation of life; therefore, there must be within perfection an internal activity. At the same time it should also be a community. For that reason, there must be a manifestation of the activity. We can regard this behavior as depending throughout, not on imperfection, but solely on the idea of the communal life. That leads us to distinguish between two kinds of behavior. There is, on the one hand, the behavior that refers plainly to happiness and which cares nothing about the result, as it desires only to express the inner life (therefore one that only "expresses"). On the other hand, there is the kind of behavior that is mainly efficacious and, according as it is motivated by pleasure [*Lust*] or pain [*Unlust*], it appears as opposing imperfection or moving toward perfection.

THE IMPULSE TO ACTION MODIFIED BY PLEASURE OR PAIN

How do these two forms of behavior stand in relation to Christian ethics? Which is its true subject? Here again we must assume that Christian ethics has to do with the present situation of the Christian church. In that case we cannot proceed exclusively from happiness as the situation of perfection. However, do we have absolutely nothing to do here with this? For, if the behavior that Christian ethics should describe were occasioned merely by the situation of imperfection, then only efficacious activity could be its content. In order to decide whether this alone belongs to

Christian ethics or whether the other type of behavior is also included, we must return to the true fundamental situation of the Christian as such and to the church as such. If we wish to take up the matter there, we will always have to say: If we imagine the Christian church as the kingdom of God on earth, then we must posit something contemporary in opposition to it, for the whole human race is surely one but not yet entirely within the Christian church. A part of the human race, therefore, is passed over. Naturally, that stimulates activity. Let us suppose that what we earlier called the perception of deficiency enters the picture and that we ask what we should call the situation in which we find ourselves while we are actually *in* this situation. In that case we must say that it is pain, an unpleasant feeling to those members of the human race that have been passed over. The pain, however, is not happiness. This perception of deficiency moves us to action. This can only happen, however, by virtue of the consciousness of a power within us to remedy the deficiency. The consciousness of power is obviously the antithesis to pain, and it is therefore the pleasant consciousness, the pleasure of spiritual content. Is this pleasure happiness? Precisely speaking, this must be denied; for insofar as the consciousness of power originates only in the consciousness of deficiency, it is not that perfect satisfaction that arises purely from the inner life. This pleasure cannot be conceived except as conditioned by pain, and therefore it cannot possibly be happiness. For that same reason, this pain cannot be termed complete unhappiness, since the possibility of perceiving the pain already presupposes a kind of perfection. Also, that pleasure in itself is obviously something that we must conceive throughout, not as always the same, but as now greater, now smaller. Thus it is marked by unevenness, requiring a more and less, which is also not happiness. Happiness is, therefore, neither pleasure nor pain in and of itself. Is there, in our present situation, anything other than this pleasure or this pain?

JOY IN CHRIST AND
COMMUNION WITH THE WORLD

Accordingly, we must say that there is a third type by which both of these are qualified and which is their common foundation. What should be attained through redemption is nothing other than the communion with God, an essentially universal Christian expression meaning that the consciousness of God is a constant companion of our own consciousness, both together in harmony. To be sure, as we observe our situation in this connection in any one specific moment, we will perceive either that character of pleasure or that of pain, according as we see that harmony strengthened or weakened. However, if we abstract from the specific content of a particular moment, and if we are .conscious of ourselves to the extent that in our common consciousness our separation from God has been overcome, and therefore if we observe life apart from changes in it, then the awareness of this fundamental situation, apart from the temporal differences, is obviously happiness. Because we are aware that this has originated through the influence of Christ, it is happiness in Christ or joy in Christ. This appears, however, in temporal content sometimes more as pleasure, sometimes more as pain. If we in the Christian church, on the one hand, think of this happiness as the fundamental situation in general, and, at the same time, regard it as in relation to and in communion with the world, what is it then that produces the consciousness of pleasure? Naturally, every positive consciousness of power stimulates the search for the extent to which one can transcend the antithesis and be effective in the world. What will be the natural result if we, on the other hand, think of this as pain? Obviously, there will arise the consciousness that we do not stand entirely on one side of the antithesis, and then will come the longing to transcend it. Each has its ground, not in happiness in and of itself, but in its contrary

75

modifications. Therefore, on the one hand, I put myself in touch with what I can stir up with my power, and, on the other hand, I put myself in touch with something that can influence me by its power.

Is there absolutely no behavior produced from the consciousness of happiness in and of itself? Surely that which aims toward the idea of life as a community, toward the circulation of expressions of life and their communication.

Now the issue is this: Here we have two different behaviors, which exist only as a pair and which exhaust the activity of the Christian church in its present situation. For if the behavior which arises from the alternation of pleasure and pain is not present in the church, then it must not have appropriated its relationship to life nor even comprehended its community. Now we can judge the major question. If we say that the perfection of the Christian resides in absolute rest—i.e., quietism—that would contain, first of all, a total abstraction of the relationship between the Christian church and the world, i.e., the church militant. Can that proceed from the perfection of the Christian? Returning in this activity to the archetypal image of Christ, we must say that if Christ had also abstracted from the relationship to the world, then redemption should not have occurred and we would find in that activity only dissimilarity with Christ. In that case, absolute rest should be understood as excluding that behavior which proceeds from the inner life seeking to communicate itself. Then quietism is the most complete form of separatism. However, it was Christ's intention that the disciples should be in union.

From this it follows that we must consider both kinds of behaviors in the sphere of Christian ethics but certainly not as identical to each other. The one is essentially timeless and belongs simply to the idea of the common life. The other, however, depends upon the task to be accomplished in historical life, such that the task and the behavior are continually diminished over the course of time, although without either ever reaching zero so long as there is any temporal life at all. From this it follows, clearly, that if we cannot separate the common life from human nature in the present situation, and if at all times, so long as the antithesis of pleasure and pain persists in our consciousness, an external incentive to action is the fundamental nature of the thing, it is impossible to separate Christian piety from action, a proposition which very often is misunderstood and assailed. It also follows from what has been said that we already have an indication of the division of our whole presentation inasmuch as we have found two different types of behavior. It is by no means clear *eo ipso* whether this distinction would also be the sharpest. We must still investigate that, but we must first dispose of one difficulty.

RELATIONSHIP OF THE PARTICULAR TO THE UNIVERSAL FORMULA

If one must now concede that existence and life in the Christian community cannot be conceived apart from behavior that proceeds from it, a second question arises: Is this behavior the same in everything that belongs to the Christian community such that a description of the behavior can be contained in a universal formula? Although it can appear dangerous, we have already conceded that we cannot establish a universal Christian ethics without offering something vague and unsatisfactory and that we must limit ourselves to Protestant ethics. What lies outside the Protestant church, and is therefore omitted here, belongs chiefly to the Roman Catholic Church. What was mixed together prior to the Reformation was separated in the Reformation, and there were many things prior to the Reformation that accorded with the Protestant type and many that corresponded with the Catholic. Thus Christian ethics branches off already. Catholic ethics is one thing in connection to the disposition of the Christian life and the Protestant something else. Can one not go still further and break it down even more? For example, if we consider the enormous divide between supernaturalism and rationalism, we can hardly think that both could establish identical ethics. The prescriptions of each one must have different motivations. It will be necessary, therefore, to explain on which of the two sides our ethics will stand. However, one could go still further and say: Christian ethics also has to include how the life and behavior of human beings are determined in their other relationships—this may not be entirely disregarded. There the form of the whole external life itself comes to speech, and someone can say: An ethics must have a different form for monarchical or republican models, and then the most important thing is how the Christian community is related to the other dimensions of life. Thus ethics will again differ for a church community, depending upon whether it is subordinate to the state, or whether it is free, or whether it has subordinated the state to itself. The most striking thing is this question: Can the moral behavior of one person be the same as that of another? Are there not continuous instances where one person behaves this way and another behaves that way, and both are right? Certainly there would also be instances where everyone must behave in the same way regardless of their differences. However, if we ask how one sphere of behavior is related to the other, we will hardly say that the sphere where each behaves in his own way completely disappears. If we should dismiss this entirely, ethics becomes something very indeterminate, because a large portion of human life does not allow itself to be ordered like that. To what extent should we find here both an area of freedom and a secure boundary? One cannot deny that both are true, unless one also denies that human beings are different, and surely that cannot be done. How does it stand, therefore, on this view regarding the universality [*Allgemeinheit*] of Christian ethics? If we admit that, one sees that there is in all concrete human actions something that is so simply because the person is such a person and not another. May universal prescriptions be given for this? No, because it would presuppose that this distinctive character can be circumscribed by a definite formula, and that is a contradiction.

Within what boundary then must we enclose it? In relation to those things in human behavior which have their roots in the distinctive character of the individual, there is no judge other than the individual himself. In this view, he can only be his own judge but in no way his own teacher—that is, it will not easily be the case that one can say in advance, here I will behave this way according to my character while another of a different character will behave that way. However, that is not possible. In this case there is no prescription; rather, each one is his own judge only after the fact. Now we must say: In this case there is nothing else to do but to refer each individual to his conscience, and this means: Do that which Christian ethics teaches, but always as it summons your individuality. But no one can also *Barth* claim that this distinctiveness stands, in all respects, in the same relationship to behavior itself; rather, we can imagine here a relative antithesis. For example, one imagines oneself capable of fulfilling something in a contract with someone else which is conditioned by the content of the contract. Surely, in that case, the distinctive element will be minimal. On the other hand, one imagines that a person should choose his own vocation. Then we must admit that if this is already settled in definite terms by a contract, the action is just that. However, where there is nothing of the sort, there can be nothing else but the whole distinctive character of the person that determines this decision. Here, therefore, the distinctive element is clearly at its maximum. If we keep an eye on the antithesis, what can we say regarding the possibility of a complete ethics except this: Wherever we further analyze a specific point in our theories, we must understand correctly the relationship of the individual to what has already been decided by universal reckoning? One can do no more than this. If we can master this worst case where the universal rule seems to disappear, then the other, which concerns the splintering of the Christian church into different classes, creates less difficulty for us. But even here the way must be marked.

We will certainly have to single out what belongs primarily to the Protestant church. Protestant ethics surely has its characteristic sphere. In each mode of action there will be something that has its ground in its distinctive character. We therefore intentionally limit our ethics to the Protestant church, but we always want both to compare the two (Protestant and Catholic) and to ground the Protestant ethics in universal Christian ethics. That can happen only to the extent that we become conscious ourselves, through a description of actions, of our differences from the Roman Catholic Church.

THE SIGNIFICANCE OF "DOGMATIC" DIFFERENCES FOR ETHICS

How does it stand, however, with the antitheses within the Protestant church? Strictly speaking, the Protestant church is not an external unity such that one could say, generally, that all who differentiate themselves from the religious confession of the Catholics would likewise be the same. One cannot say that. This disunity is found in theory and practice. In dogmatic theology this difference has led in part to the division of the church community. Thus the question is whether division that touches upon a difference of theory in dogmatics will also have a bearing on ethics. If we now look carefully at the differences within the Protestant church itself, it is easy to see that no obvious relationship exists between the differences in dogmatics and ethics. For example, if we observe the difference between the Reformed and Lutheran branches of Protestantism, each will say that the statement of doctrine concerning the Lord's Supper can have no bearing on ethics. Similarly, each will claim that the difference in the doctrine of predestination, which appears to have a bearing on ethics, is based on a misunderstanding. One must say that according to Reformed doctrine, behavior must

80

disappear [as a subject for ethics] since everything depends
upon God's decree; but if we consider that from the
standpoint of the influence of the Holy Spirit, then this
objection disappears. The huge dogmatic differences cited
above as genuine heresies nevertheless had no bearing on
ethics. For example, one can say that Arianism has docetic
tendencies and this has a detrimental effect on ethical
instruction, as we saw above. But this docetism was
unconscious in Arianism. We can say that, followed
consistently, the Arian view of the person of Christ must
lead to docetism. However, this logical outcome has not
ensued, and so Arianism could have no influence on ethics.
The same thing can be said of Socinianism, which does not
annul the example of Christ and claim perfect obedience.
Here again the dogmatic difference lies outside influence
on the moral. However, when we come to the antithesis
between rationalism and supernaturalism that presently
flourishes, especially in the Protestant church, it is a
different matter. Many theologians who in their theories
are completely in accord with the supernaturalistic view
have allowed themselves to be swept along by the universal
tendency, with reference to Christian ethics, that there is
little difference between their ethics and the ethics of
rationalists. However, when we return to the point that the
essential character of rationalism contains a tendency not
present in supernaturalism—namely, to loosen the specific
bonds of Christian community—we will say that is a
difference which necessarily must be manifest even in
Christian ethics. Thus as soon as one clearly establishes the
principle of Christian ethics as based upon the essential
character of the spirit governing the church, the rationalistic view must be excluded at the outset, for it must be
immediately apparent that there is indeed a higher spirit
here. The one who denies the higher spirit at this point
takes his stand upon the rationalistic view, and the
appearance of Christ is simply a means to develop further
primordial human reason and to make it more effective. In

81

that case, however, the central significance of the Christian church for ethics, and therefore the distinctive character of Christian ethics, is obliterated. Hence one must proceed from the premise that it is impossible to consider all dogmatic differences as bearing upon ethics to the same extent. Only in the case of similar dogmatic grounds will there always be agreement in ethics. There will remain a division between the Protestant and Catholic churches; and ethics will be beyond rationalism and supernaturalism.

THE ENGAGEMENT OF PIETY WITH ACTUAL POLITICAL-SOCIAL RELATIONSHIPS

Concerning the further divisions in the Protestant church itself, it has indeed been said that a total fragmentation of the church community will not be caused by the individual dogmatic points in dispute as long as there is no difference of spirit present. In that case, it is natural that the spirit must have influence on ethics, and the influence must be developed there. The point is this: It cannot be denied that at the first meetings of the Swiss, Saxonist, and other theologians, especially at the Marburg Colloquy, both parties seemed strange to each other and attributed that to different spirits; but observing the matter closely, it led, nevertheless, to nothing other than the different relationships in which the reformers stood to the government and to worldly power, and then to the different character that the reformers also attributed to civil activity. Therefore, it is only a difference generated by the relationship of the church to the state, without any difference in piety itself. Christian piety must express itself in all connections as appropriate for its relationships. The diverse relationships, however, are, as above, to be considered as individual entities, because they are all different, and thus the individual entities will have to be considered just like each individual generally. It is wrong to assume that a deeper dogmatic reason was necessarily the occasion for the division, since at that time it was only the *doctrine* of the sacrament, which was already present before as the bond of the church community, that came to speech. Since, therefore, the dogmatic distinctions are such that they can have no bearing on Christian ethics, and on the other hand, rationalism and supernaturalism are present in both church communities, thus, clearly, the one must be hidden behind the other.

EXPANSIONS AND ADVANCEMENTS

There is still something else to consider with regard to the universality of Christian ethics. We have already conceded that Christianity is to be understood as an historical entity undergoing periodic development and that a system of ethics can be valid only for one such era. Placing ourselves on the boundary, we now ask: How does it happen that a new era begins? Clearly not from outside, but from inside out by the activity of individuals, who, nevertheless, belong to the time in which they were brought up and by which they were shaped. However, they are those through whom something new is developed. Is such activity of the individual something immoral from which the morality of the next period develops? In political history one is inclined to agree. It is often said that historical transformations are possible only through revolutions, and that these revolutions are immoral. That must be denied; the revolutionary, to be more precise, is the one who is immoral, and without him, morality would develop in a peaceful way, as even now it has developed from the morality of the revolution. In the sphere of the church we cannot accept such a claim, because each development in it bespeaks the greater effectiveness of the divine Spirit. The actions can be immoral only if they continue solely in what was present earlier. In that case it should be said that the greatest effect is derived from a situation in which the divine Spirit was repressed. There is still a duplicity present here to which we have not yet given close attention. If we observe the progress of the Christian life in some peaceful situation and consider the two distinctive kinds of behavior, then we must say that the self-expressive behavior of the individual manifests the whole situation of the church as it is; and it is, strictly speaking, a behavior of the whole, of which the individual is merely an agent. The same is true of efficacious behavior when one thinks of a peaceful time. This is evoked by imperfection, but this again is illuminated by the perfection already present in the church or even by the consciousness of power that is already there. In that sense, therefore, this arises from nothing new and also aspires to nothing new. However, if an improvement in the whole should originate from actions of the individual, that is a behavior of the individual on the whole, and it expresses what is in him and should be made manifest. There could be no historical development if there were no such persons. Should we, for that reason, say that they stand above Christian ethics? It was said above that a system of Christian ethics can materialize only in such a peaceful situation because during upheavals no new ethics can be created. However, it does not follow from this that each person in such a situation can test his actions by a universal principle, nor does it follow that these were not a part of Christian ethics. Christian ethics is the standard for such actions, but that does not damage its universality. In every part of the ethics we must inquire about this difference.

We must return here to the Christian consciousness as it is the permanent ground of Christian actions. Whenever the individual acts as one manifesting the whole and as the effective organ of the whole, his consciousness is totally identified with the consciousness of the whole, and he acts in the name of the whole, and his situation is then one of a living and effective communal feeling. However, if some-

84

thing that should attain to universal life and thought stirs in an individual, he must perceive the difference between himself and the whole. In that case, therefore, his consciousness is purely personal and stands in opposition to the consciousness of the whole. Each advance of the whole can proceed only from actions of the latter type; those which come from the first type are only a diffusion, but certainly not an actual advancement of the whole. Therefore, we must also take that into consideration. Here again we find ourselves at a point of significant difference between the Roman Catholic and Protestant churches in practice and theory. Since in the Roman Catholic Church morality rests entirely upon obedience to the church, it has, strictly speaking, no room for such progressive behavior, and it permits only such advances as proceed from an official representative. That can certainly not be the case for us. We do not establish such specific distinctions between clergy and laity, which is the only form under which the Catholic Church can seek advancement. The whole significance of this will become clear if one further observation is made.

IDENTIFICATION WITH THE WHOLE AND OPPOSING POINTS OF VIEW

Often, something can obtain in many regions of the church but not in others. When it develops there, it nevertheless begins as something new. The situation, therefore, where one is placed in opposition to the whole in order to give validity to something new is not a rare occurrence. If the modification of the theoretical idea is mentioned and if this proceeds from an individual, that is nevertheless always a moral action and belongs to the same kind, because from his point of view he opposes that which was hitherto valid in his circle. That always happens, and there must certainly be prescriptions for it. However, the important thing is not whether that which somebody desires to set up is really better or not. Because the one on whom this presses must nevertheless act, be it right or wrong. Here we can, in part, state the matter generally and say: It is a twofold relationship, which must be viewed as universal, that there are, on the one hand, actions for each individual in which he is identified entirely with the whole. To that belongs a number of improvements which each makes in himself or in others, that is, if the principle that one sets up is already operative. On the other hand, however, we must assume as a universal possibility that each can enter into a situation of placing himself against that which is valid for the whole. For both situations we must have prescriptions. This is something distinctive to Protestant ethics. The Roman Catholic Church, for that reason, makes the reproach that here the ground of division has been constitutionally established. It says: In our case the individual has no other principle than obedience to the church. By that he is denied opposition to the whole. One wants to say that there can be no improvement in the church itself, because by means of the doctrine of infallibility it declares that everything is already perfect. In the case of real transformations it is the church guided by the Holy Spirit that causes these. Obviously, on our side is a free life that is clearly not present in the Roman Catholic Church, but which, nevertheless, is not constituted as arbitrariness. This is simply the immediate effect of the primordial principle in each individual. The Roman Catholic Church says, on the other hand, that if there is something to be established it happens through the divine Spirit in the congregation. If we say that in a situation where an individual perceives and establishes relative opposition that he should act according to the prescriptions of Scripture, it is precisely according to the divine Spirit that he acts. Because the Scripture passages pertain to him, he is governed by them; and then if we observe how it has always happened in the representative events of the church, we find that results have issued only from those in opposition. Thus the divine Spirit, nevertheless, cannot have worked this way in the one and that way in the other. The more one wants to fix the activity of the divine Spirit in individuals, the more it becomes evident that that is an illusion.

ELIMINATING THE DEBATES OVER THE PRINCIPLE OF ETHICS AND THE CAPACITY FOR MORAL BEHAVIOR

Now we have reached the point where we can determine the whole order of our method from these variations.

First we must consider two things that are included in other ethics: (1) the essential aim of morality and (2) the essential ability to be moral.

The first means that the principle of ethics should be — deduced as in rational ethics. The second concerns the doctrine of the freedom of the will.

If a person is told that he should behave in one way or another, he must first be convinced that he can behave in this way. However, one can and must dispense entirely with these discussions. That is to say: We regard Christian ethics as the description of those ways of acting that have evolved in the Christian church from the effect of the Christian principle. Because we have now abandoned the imperative form, we no longer have cause to say, "You should for that reason" and so on. Those who continue in the customary way will consider this a ruse to circumvent the fact that human beings will not act with ultimate motives of morality, that they abandon the imperative form. Nevertheless, one must acknowledge that Christian ethics is a reality only for the Christian church. If someone demands that I tell him in each individual instance the reasons why he must act in such and such a way, he is told: To declare that is not the issue here. Whoever is in the Christian church knows it. Whoever does not feel a part of it leaves. Motives do not have to be mentioned at all. However, when someone is first moved to enter the Christian church, it is certainly not right to confront him immediately with Christian ethics. What then could one accept as a principle? Happiness and rationality are not concepts that, in and of themselves, belong to the complex of Christian ethics. Whoever engages in this has already passed from Christian ethics to rational ethics. However, if we proceed from the authentically religious sphere, we must employ the idea of "the highest essence" and always say that a person in harmony with God cannot behave otherwise than this way or that, or that this and that is the divine will. The first is the descriptive form and already excludes a broader motive. Can one properly establish motives in the Christian church such that someone *wants* to carry out the will of God? No. Nobody needs a motivation except someone not yet in the Christian church. Therefore, we can be spared this entirely. Instead, the universal ground is to be laid down in a general formula which in each case enters consciousness as a universal Christian principle.

The second consideration is the discussion of moral capacity. Here, generally speaking, the matter depends heavily on one's view of Christianity. One who has a completely naturalistic view of Christianity is in the same situation with Christian ethics as with the establishment of rational ethics. However, the corollary is that in this view there lies an ever present tendency to ignore the Christian community. We have already excluded, *eo ipso*, such a naturalistic view. On the opposite side, there are still a great variety of views in which an investigation into moral capacity is necessary. What Schleiermacher here takes as fundamental and considers, as it were, a dogmatic proposition grounding Christian ethics is this: Through Christ and by his own testimony and the corresponding testimony of Christians from the earliest period onward, an active power has entered the Christian church. This power is designated the divine Spirit, and this is the moral capacity that is at the

88

same time effective in the Christian church. If we presuppose this and also presuppose that such faith cannot endure without accepting this essential effective power, then moral capacity is already assumed and no further investigation is necessary. It might be objected that this principle should deal with the question of whether or not I can, but this will receive the following answer: It is clear from this that this principle is still very weak in you. The further question—How should I strengthen it?—surely does not belong to Christian ethics. To answer this, even though we are digressing, we must say that here there can be no other way than via the original impulse. One cannot strengthen the principle on one's own, for that power lies in the divine Word. In the individual there must be two different things, an autonomous activity as well as an impressionable nature. Thus one must say to him: You can do nothing to change that. When you yourself have a struggle with that, I can give you nothing further. It is already a sign of progress when you have the struggle. Remain in the living community with grace, just as one must abide in communion with nature in order to live; and out of the Word be self-actualizing, and then this autonomous activity will grow by itself in this community.

Surely, therefore, we only damage the cause of Christianity when we try to answer such questions in Christian ethics.

THE DIFFERENCE BETWEEN THE CHURCH MILITANT AND THE CHURCH TRIUMPHANT

Now the important thing is (1) to establish a general formula which so expresses the essence of the Christian community that this expression remains present in all other formulas that are developed from it, and (2) to classify the behavior in such a way that we are convinced that we have staked out the whole sphere of behavior.

Our point of departure was the dogmatic difference between the church militant and the church triumphant. We said that there is in the church militant a behavior that is also present in the church triumphant, but there is also in the former a distinctive behavior not found in the latter. We have already distinguished these: (1) a behavior which proceeds from the Christian consciousness under the form of pleasure and searches immediately for a subject to which the pleasure is actively manifested, and (2) a behavior that proceeds from pain. The first is nothing but the expression and communication of what is internal, and we have called it "self-expressive" behavior. The latter we have termed "efficacious" behavior, since it wants to effect changes that will overcome the difference between the church militant and the church triumphant.

This, therefore, is the major division. Now concerning the establishment of a general formula, there is more to be said in terms of how much value one puts on this. Schleiermacher seeks the conceptual form throughout, but little attention is given to the establishment of the general principle. Here especially, for Schleiermacher, the organization of the whole is the main point, but it is from this that the conceptual form must be perceived. In the case of the general formula one can conceive of many varied possibilities. It is above all a twofold reality, and it is a matter of indifference which of the two one embraces.

THE TWO FOCAL POINTS OF CHRISTIAN ETHICS

After all that has been said, it is not necessary to say much about the fact that everything depends upon two dogmatic points. These are the doctrine of Christ and the doctrine of the Holy Spirit. The former is indeed one focal point, because Christian ethics should portray the life which is restored by Christ and which should manifest the union of the life of the believer with Christ. In the same way the doctrine of the Holy Spirit is the other focal point, for this is the power from which the Christian life arises. However, whether one or the other of these points is used preeminently to construct the one or the other form is a matter of indifference. The union of the two would also be unimportant for Schleiermacher, for neither can be conceived without the other, and each is set in and with the other. If one wants to choose a formula that explicitly combines the two, that means nothing other than setting forth explicitly the bond that already lies in each one. If, for example, one wants to say that Christian ethics should describe all human behavior that resembles the behavior of Christ, that is the principle as expressed from one point of view. If one prefers the imperative formula, the general formula will run as follows: Act such that your behavior always resembles the behavior of Christ. No one will say that something is still missing. For it is already implied that this can happen only through the Spirit of Christ. Also, if one says that Christian ethics should describe every behavior that can be portrayed as originating from the agency of the Holy Spirit in the human soul, that is also a general principle and the result would be the same. Here, the imperative form would be: Above all, act in such a way that you allow yourself to be governed exclusively by the divine Spirit. This formula is based entirely on the previous one. If one wants to draw both together, then one does, strictly speaking, only what has already been done. However, if one sought a focal point that lies outside these two, then plainly there would arise something entirely different by which the pure sphere of Christian ethics could not be entirely enclosed. Accordingly, we must conceive these formulas in equal measure as that to which we must reduce everything else.

THE ANTITHESIS BETWEEN PROTESTANT AND ROMAN CATHOLIC CHURCHES

If, however, another demand to which we have conceded a certain validity were established—namely, Christian ethics should express only the Protestant Christian life-style—one could say that these formulas were in any case universally Christian. Therefore, we would not expect to find them excluding what is distinctively Protestant. Certainly that would be a fine thing, but can we claim that in all fairness? Whoever is entirely certain that we perceive perfectly the antithesis between the Protestant and Catholic churches can rightly claim that the distinctive Protestant form must already be evident in the universal. However, Schleiermacher did not venture to maintain this, because in dogmatics and morality there are still many things in which the one has not yet been definitively separated from the other. Yes, one can affirm that in our case there are still many things in ecclesiastical life that bear a hidden contradiction to the true Protestant principle and which will appear at one time and then disappear. Presently, however, this is not yet acknowledged. If one wants to claim that this opposition has already fully developed, then one must either assume that both churches have set themselves completely apart so that each in its own distinctiveness can view the other in peace or conclude that peace between the two is not possible and each must seek to absorb the other into itself. With regard to the first assumption, it is clear that such peace does not exist, and thus it is evident that this state of affairs is not yet fully realized. With regard to the second, we cannot claim that this struggle is recognized as absolute. The two churches do not yet agree about the reciprocal relationship. The situation, therefore, is not like that. For that reason, we cannot pledge ourselves to modify the general principle of Christian ethics such that it would be adequate for every Protestant ethics. Starting with the general, we either establish a use for this principle that can only occur in the Protestant church, or, if we do not do that, it will be fairly accidental whether or not we meet up with the Protestant. Now again that would not be sufficient for our intention; for in that way the presentation would be less rigorous. Therefore, it appears that we must remain with the second. For that purpose we already have guidance.

POSITIVE AND NEGATIVE MORALITY

In the Roman Catholic Church the only valid rule for each individual is obedience to the church, and the application of the general principle to the Roman Catholic Church will be different. It is said: In order to know what resembles Christ, you must hold to the pronouncements of ·the Roman Catholic Church. The directive in that case would be something entirely external. One would seek descriptive rubrics under which to place the prescriptions of the church. Now the question is: Can we place something positive over against this? We have said: Every Protestant Christian is not referred absolutely in his life to the commands of the church but to that which, for him, on the basis of Scripture, is clearly the divine will. Therefore, concerning the character of individual actions, we are certain that we will set forth what is purely Protestant if we refer everyone to one's conscience as it is formed by Scripture. The one as well as the other can always be understood in a twofold way, and from that arise two different types of morality, one more negative and the other more positive. The Catholic principle can be expounded as follows: Whenever you want to do something, you first ask what the command of the church is in this connection. The principle derived from the Protestant church is set forth as follows: Never act without first consulting your conscience, which is formed by Scripture. Schleiermacher calls both of these negative morality, and one cannot stop with them. If no mention is made here of the source of the motive for behavior, and if one must assume that human beings are not yet perfect, then certainly there can arise impulses to actions that are contrary to the divine will. If a person questions his conscience before acting, he will not permit himself to do that. However, it does not follow that he will do those deeds which would be generated by the divine Spirit if it were strongly present in him. Therefore, the directive would be only from outside, thus similar to the Catholic position, and the main point would be simply what is forbidden and what is commanded. However, the Protestant principle can also be understood as follows: We think of the divine Spirit as actually governing human beings, and we describe all actions that can originate in life if the divine Spirit gives the impulse. Thus the description is not determined by something different.

If we hold to this and take it to its conclusion, we must be sure to include all types of action that can arise at all from the agency of the divine Spirit. In this way, the directive is not something external for us. To be sure, such a positive morality can also be conceived in the Roman Catholic Church, as when one imagines each individual driven by living obedience to the church and the actions as a result of that. In that case, the established principle is by itself the effective power. However, because this is nothing more than simply the disposition of obedience, it must get its substance from outside after all.

THE SIGNIFICANCE OF THE DOCTRINE OF THE CHURCH FOR THE ORGANIZATION OF ETHICS

Therefore, concerning our arrangement, we could not have found its foundation anywhere else but in the doctrine of the Christian church. If we put ourselves back in the situation where Christian ethics was not yet separated from theology, the individual propositions of Christian theology can be presented as corollaries at any suitable point. However, let us consider this: As far as this situation is concerned, the basic idea was to organize Christian ethics for itself without external causes, and if we ask ourselves where in dogmatics is the point that gives occasion to it, no one will deny that it is the ✓ article on the Christian church. As we have already said: The Christian church is, on the one hand, the church militant, i.e., the church set in opposition to the world; and, on the other hand, it is the church triumphant, i.e., the church purely manifesting communion with God. These are not merely two different situations but two different relationships already in the present situation. Also, Christian behavior must itself vary according to these two major relationships, and from them the classifications of efficacious and self-expressive behavior arise. Therefore, with the help of the derived formula appropriate to the Protestant church, we must search still further in each of these two spheres of behavior for the guidance of the general principle. The behavior shows itself partially as communicating, as expressing a stimulation which it has, and partially, according to whether the Christian consciousness contains pleasure or pain, as appropriating or repulsing behavior. The former we must affirm even in the ✓ perfected church, the latter merely in the church militant.

The division we have made appears, on the one hand, as a dichotomy; but, on the other hand, it can be seen as a trichotomy. This apparent ambiguity dissolves when we consider the following: According to form, the dichotomy is obviously dominant in the doctrine of the church as well as in the essential difference in the primordial consciousness. In the doctrine of the church the dichotomy expresses itself with total certainty; but in the reduction to the difference it is also there in the form, because the opposition between pleasure and pain is subordinate if one recalls the greater difference—namely, that the higher consciousness should be conceived in and for itself, but that as the higher consciousness it is also modified over time. Thus we have to distinguish two different things in the object of Christian ethics, self-expressive behavior and efficacious behavior, the latter pointed toward an external goal. Only as a subheading under efficacious behavior would there be set forth the divisions between that which has its ground in the Christian consciousness as pleasure and that which has it as pain.

When we look at the real world, the matter appears otherwise, and the trichotomy could be the most useful. In the real world one readily prefers to look upon equal quantities as much as possible and is likely to find there that the self-expressive behavior would not be equal to efficacious behavior in those terms. But we can be satisfied if one major part of efficacious behavior approaches equality in terms of quantity. Therefore, in the actual procedure we can always treat the two major parts of efficacious activity as one.

THE PRIORITY OF THE CHRISTIAN LIFE OVER CHRISTIAN ETHICS

Still more questions of greater significance arise that only catch the eye when we see the relationship of this classification and the formula to be developed to individual actions. Strictly speaking, the individual discrete actions have nothing to do with us. Christian ethics should give only a complete and ordered overview of everything that belongs to the Christian life. It is, to be sure, a common opinion, which one finds even in rational ethics, that ethics should serve to bring forth moral actions. That is, however, entirely mistaken. It is certainly clear that ethical instruction as such, the complex of formulas of moral behavior, cannot, generally speaking, bring forth moral actions because moral actions are always prior to ethics. Ethics is also never a matter of the whole but something conceptually rigorous, therefore belonging to only a small part of the whole and the property of a small group. The Christian life, however, should be represented in its totality. Therefore, in supporting the common opinion that ethics should bring forth moral actions, we would again be siding with the Catholic Church, where ethics precedes the moral life of the laity, because the prescriptions of the clergy must be derived from the ethics. Nevertheless, even there, the action itself is independent of ethics, because one acts only out of obedience to the church and not because ethics wills it. For that reason, one can never accede to such an immediate relationship between ethics and morality. The use of ethics in life commences when something is disputed and the morality of an individual cannot define itself at some time or other; or still later, if the individual action is already completed, ethics can be used to test it. One must take the phrase "to be completed" in a broader sense, however. Here we call the action "completed" when the concept of "the purpose" is already fixed for the particular situation, and when the resolve whence the behavior springs is also present. Only here can one examine the action. However, it is inverted logic to extract the elements of behavior from the ethics. One must accept then two kinds of moral persons: (1) those who were moral before there was ethics or to whom it was not known, and (2) those who have the instruction, which again in our sphere would be Catholic.

THE CONFLICT OF DUTIES: CONCEPTUAL AND TEMPORAL

Now, however, there is still another question. It is said that one could manage to bring forth the moral actions without ethics if everything goes so smoothly; but if the duties conflict, then one could not exist without ethics. Thus, its vocation would be to resolve the conflict of duties. The most important thing is what is properly designated as "conflict of duties." The matter is entirely simple: Let us say, it occurs to me that I should do this and that. However, since I have this consciousness, I also have, conjointly, the sense that I should perhaps do something else. When these conflict with each other, then we have the conflict of duties. The main point, however, is whether these two formulas to which I have referred are contradictory conceptually or only in reference to the moment.

If there were actual duties that conflicted conceptually with each other, there would be neither morality nor ethics. For example, it is said that there is a duty of resistance, even if it demands the sacrifice of life, or possibly a duty of action also with the sacrifice of life; on the other hand, there is the duty of self-preservation. The two can never appear simultaneously in the consciousness; rather, one must either forget one of them or deliberately behave contrary to it. One could at least say that here an uncertainty pervades the sphere of morality. In general, whenever such formulas appear, there is no ethical definition, and many ethicists have decided that in certain instances all ethics cease. As soon as we accept this and say that the concept of morality does not encompass the whole of life, then morality has in this way been transcended. Either everything is moral conceptually or nothing is. Only where there is no activity of the will is there no need for morality.

of tragedy

One only has to choose between the concept of morality in general and the concept of conflict. Conflict should, however, already presuppose ethics, and that presents a problem. Conflict should not lie in the theory; in other words, of the formulas that stand in such a relationship to each other, one must always be false, else the moral life itself is a contradiction.

If outside the theory we observe one who falls into such a conflict, he has no clear consciousness for one or the other. We must, therefore, in determining the formulas, proceed in such a way that no such conflict enters. How that is to be accomplished will here be left undecided. Granted, the genuine conflict of duties is not present in the concept;

rather all forms have been established such that there is no contradiction. Many things clash with each other, not conceptually but with regard to time. Thus the second type of conflict arises in relation to the moment. Is this conflict just as invalid as the former? Certainly, but for the completely opposite reason. This conflict must be permanent, because in the moment we can do only one thing, yet each moment includes the whole of morality. In this way, there could never be a good conscience in ethical practice if this conflict were not eliminated; however, it is also invalid for another reason. But how is this conflict related to our task, which is concerned only with theory? This conflict in no way affects our task (e.g., justice and charity). The first is concerned, among other things, with paying one's debts. Should someone, therefore, always pay his debts before being charitable? No. This conflict, however, in no way affects the theory. The main distinction—i.e., the contradiction between duties conceptually and the conflict of various duties in relation to the moment—must definitely be maintained. We even have formulas already established.

We must, therefore, always test our formulas to see if they are also correct. Then, it is also true that if the mere presupposition satisfies us, we can accept responsibility with greater certainty since we can point out that in what we established as the complex of the Christian life no conflict of duties is present.

THE EFFICACIOUS ELEMENTS IN SELF-EXPRESSIVE BEHAVIOR, AND VICE VERSA

When our classification is complete and we can point out that it allows no occasion for such contradiction, then we will be certain. The question is how, in relation to such contradiction, our major classes of action are related to each other whereby it must be assumed that our classification is

99

exhaustive. Concerning the first type, the matter rests as follows: we must say that every particular action will belong in all of our major divisions taken together, and only *a potiori* [with greater reason] can it belong exclusively to one of them. When we consider our classification as a dichotomy, we can say that every self-expressive behavior will be simultaneously an efficacious behavior, and vice versa. Herein lies what has just been expressed. It depends, therefore, only on the vindication of these propositions and on the establishment of similar propositions in relation to the subdivisions. If we return once more to that on which the classification is based, then each efficacious activity will be that through which the Christian principle, already effective in an individual, has already appropriated something of what has been given to him, as it were, as material. In other words, if we return to our original presentation of the Christian life and at the same time consider carefully its goal—the church triumphant, from which we have excluded all efficacious behavior—we still must consider that the whole of human nature should be fully permeated by the Christian principle, and then no external consequence could result from it. In that sense, all behavior belongs under the rubric of efficacious behavior. If we take this explanation as fundamental, we will have to concede that each efficacious behavior is at the same time a self-expressive behavior. For, because this is an activity directed outward, it contains within itself the fact that the active principle appears in the external and enters into the other and brings forth a result. Therefore, it is always a self-expressive behavior first and then an efficacious behavior. The self-expressive is only a means to the efficacious, however. Conversely, the self-expressive life is also an efficacious life. That holds true only for self-expressive behavior in the sphere of the church militant, where the goal is still to be realized. The self-expressive behavior depends on this: Human life is always life in community and the consciousness of this community also belongs to the human consciousness. For that reason, we also attribute essentially to the church triumphant, which holds within itself the complete union of human nature with the Christian principle, such a self-expressive behavior. Because of this, every such movement of life becomes an outward protrusion because the community of life is concerned with communication. Now, however, let us set this self-expressive lifestyle in the church militant, in which this union of the divine principle with humanity has not been fully achieved in any particular member. If we take these both together, a self-expressive behavior will be an efficacious behavior in relation to the self-expressive, because the inner godliness of the individual can become external only through his psychic and corporeal organism. Therefore an activity is generated in the individual. Now, however, if it is an essential element of human nature that each mode of action is made easier by repetition, then it follows that the psychic and bodily organism both receives and transmits the impulse of the divine Spirit. Therein lies the fact that the influence of the divine principle is efficacious, and thus the self-expressive behavior automatically turns into an efficacious behavior. If we look at the recipient, the same thing happens, since that movement is communicated by his apprehension of the other, and the activity is strengthened because in this act of communication and apprehension both are conceived as one. Every self-expressive behavior is *a potiori per accidens* an efficacious behavior. It is impossible, therefore, for these two types of action, which mutually accompany and complement each other, to contradict each other.

THE SUBORDINATE DICHOTOMY: DISSEMINATING AND CORRECTIVE BEHAVIOR

Now we shall examine the subordinate dichotomy. We have classified efficacious behavior into that which arises from the Christian consciousness as the consciousness of power and that which arises from the Christian consciousness as pain. Now we have said: The consciousness of power proceeds naturally to seek a subject for the activity of power. This activity can be nothing other than bringing the subject into union with the principle. That is to say, it is a behavior whereby a subject that is not yet in union with the principle should be brought into union with it, or whereby an incomplete union is made more nearly complete. This behavior through which the dominion of the principle is increased in a positive way we will call "disseminating" [*verbreitend*] behavior.

The Christian consciousness, on the other hand, is experienced as pain when the movement of life appears hemmed in and when something conflicts with the Christian principle. Underlying this, therefore, is the assumption of a positive contradiction which exists essentially in the tension between that which has already appropriated the principle and that which has not. Here, then, is a relationship that must be corrected. It is a dissonance between the principle and that which should be its organ. If we designate this as "corrective" [*correctiv*] behavior, the name will reflect its general character.

Is it also the case here that a behavior of the former type [disseminating] would be at the same time, *per accidens*, the latter [corrective]? If we proceed on that basis, we encounter the problem of overcoming a positive contradiction, and this can happen anew only by an activity set in motion in human nature by the divine Spirit. Otherwise, there would be no organization. In corrective behavior we find the same character that we found in self-expressive behavior. The corrective behavior then is also, at the same time, a positive efficacious behavior, because it is strengthened by repetition. Seeing that the contradiction has been partially transcended, the receptiveness of the human spirit has to resolve the contradiction. Therefore, this behavior will be manifest as intensive "expansive" [*erweiternd*] behavior. If we consider the positive efficacious behavior, we must say: If that can be present only in the church militant, this imperfection must really exist everywhere and in each moment. Therefore, it must also be present in the consciousness, if only in an obscure way. However, the contradiction must at the same time be transcended by that.

THE EXHAUSTIVENESS OF THE CLASSIFICATION IN THE TYPES OF BEHAVIOR DERIVED FROM THE CHURCH MILITANT AND THE CHURCH TRIUMPHANT

Thus the idea of a contradiction between the various parts is entirely false. Therefore, our complete conviction that such a conflict does not occur in the Christian life still depends solely on whether the whole of our classification has been established. Strictly speaking, that can be established only through the achievement itself. There is no third concept beyond the church militant and the church triumphant. If these are dealt with exhaustively, then our task is done. We can, however, also demonstrate that one cannot conceive of a behavior other than these mentioned that would remain Christian. The two concepts should merge into one, and for that reason, it can only be conceived that either one or the other is true. A third relationship between the two is inconceivable.

In general, therefore, we are safe from this conflict, but we must still avoid its appearance in the formulas.

THE RESOLUTION OF CONFLICT

To what extent and how can it belong to the task of Christian ethics to establish formulas by which the individual can make decisions with respect to a particular moment? Every moment contains a conflict, and the completely healthy Christian life consists everywhere of the establishing and overcoming of such conflict. Therefore, if we wish to establish a rule here, we must derive it on the basis of how the peaceful improvement from one moment to the next can be the same as the constant oscillation between the establishment and the settlement of conflict. Strictly speaking, this problem is posed in each moment, but we are concerned with the solution of a problem only in one particular moment. The more completely the task of promoting the kingdom of God in its totality dawns in my consciousness in the particular action, the more nearly complete is the purity and clarity of the internal harmony. On the other hand, all parts of the moral task should be present to us at the same time, and we do one while disregarding the other. What really matters, therefore, is this conviction: While I am concentrating on one aspect of morality, other aspects are in no way affected by that.

If we actually had to do everything in each moment, then it would be impossible for us to advance toward a plan in order to implement it. Thus neither is it true now. The totality of the ethical task is to be resolved only in infinite time and thus in each moment only successively. If we imagine, therefore, a summons to a specific action and I satisfy the action, then the matter is settled and I continue on. In which situation have I been right or wrong in this process? When someone says later: You should have done this instead of that, I say: That is true, but it did not occur to me. Then the wrong does not lie in the deed but in the fact that it did not occur to me at the time. One is best protected against this if everything that falls into one's ethical sphere is always present to him. Then I can remember it, but I can have my reasons not to do it. However, I can also have the conviction that I, by doing just this, have come closest to the whole of the ethical task. A perfect harmony of the particular moral decision with the universal decision of the moral exercise is precisely that which excludes all conflicts.

The more definite this harmony is, the less one will regret what he actually did. Naturally, however, this certainty exists only to the extent that one is cognizant of one's entire position in the moral world.

If this harmony is not present, but a summons to perform a certain action arises within me, and I am uncertain whether it would not be better to perform another action, then the question arises: How can we avoid all conflict? And second, if it does arise, how should it be settled?

We will consider the latter. When a demand for an ethical action comes to me, there is also in the ethical world something which has a claim on my activity. If diverse demands come, there are diverse claims. These are made, however, by ethical individuals; therefore these claims must have their place in several rational beings. The only decision I can make, therefore, is one in which these claims will be satisfied. Generally speaking, it depends on the verdict of reason; in the Christian view, it depends on the impulse of the divine Spirit, which is present both in them and in me.

Therefore, we can say that the one whose claim I disregard in favor of another must, if he follows the Christian spirit, be just as content with that disregard as the person whose claim I satisfy by fulfilling his claim. Thus the conflict has truly been resolved. The distinction between complete and incomplete duties does perhaps not even occur here, and at the very least it would often lead to a false conclusion. To be sure, this presupposes a similarity of practice and standard in those who compete. In the sphere of Christian ethics, when we think of the divine Spirit under the rubric of brotherly love, we will say that this can have only one rule that is always the same. Besides that, however, there is no standard that allows itself to be positioned such that the divine Spirit is stronger or weaker. An error, therefore, can certainly arise in that case. Nevertheless, for the moment the matter is correctly decided. The more those who inhabit the same sphere of life agree with reference to the handling of the moral task, the less will such conflicts surface in connection with what is to be done in the moment. The whole solution, however, rests on the fact of correspondence between an impulse that appears in me and the claim in someone else.

There are, however, some actions in which this does not appear to be the case. For example, imagine the individual engaged in multiple activities which can be performed only one at a time and which, for the most part, relate to the individual himself. When one is uncertain about what should be done in the moment, then this solution is not practical. We have, for example, various studies that we pursue simultaneously. Now, supposing that one has a free hour, the question becomes: What should he do with that? The more often this happens, the more indecision there is, and we will say: He is the best who seizes the moment with the most alacrity because he tolerates no loss of time. Therefore, where the inner self-determination is lacking in such a situation, there is deficiency of moral power in general, but nothing can be accomplished by a rule to solve the conflict in a particular instance. For a great part of life, time itself frees us from this conflict to the extent that it is ordered. One wants to say that it would be best if one shaped his entire life in such a way, since then there would not remain any occasion for conflict. That is true insofar as it is clearly the best kind of help to one who is indecisive if he so organizes his time that he always knows what he must do. Generally, however, no one will want that. Obviously it is true that if the totality of one's task is present to a person and indecisiveness is not, we will say: The most correct thing presupposes that to which one is strongly inclined, to which he first gives in, provided that his entire remaining moral position is right; and those who empathize with us will agree with that. Fundamentally, therefore, we return in a roundabout way to the same decision. If we now think back on what we established earlier, we see the same antithesis, and there must be one sphere where each has his own distinctive way of going to work in this or that situation, and another sphere in which one, with disregard for diverse individuality, can trace the problem back to one general rule. The distinction, however, from a system of established rules is unmistakable. The situation in which each has to determine his own rule must, for the most part, be analogous to the latter situation, and all other situations are analogous to the former.

From this we can determine adequately just how far to specify the rule according to which preventing or avoiding the conflict of duties belongs to ethics. Here, we do not have to deal with individual actions at all, but two different things need attention here. First, the incapability to determine oneself. This refers to a moral deficiency, and there must be a place where that which overcomes this deficiency appears as a positive moral mode of action. Second, a false determination of consciousness, which will again be transcended when the general moral consciousness awakens, is also a moral deficiency and must find its place predominantly either in the positive or negative part of efficacious behavior. The matter will reappear in the case of particular deliberations.

THE BEGINNING OF MORALITY IN THE PERCEPTION OF CONTRADICTION BETWEEN OLD AND NEW

This question remains: In which classification are the particular parts of our morality to be treated? We want to understand the classification of behaviors in terms of a trichotomy, but of course the two members that constitute one member in the dichotomous classification may not be separated. What reason do we have for placing the efficacious behavior or the self-expressive behavior first or last?

The nature of the issue does not dictate with which of the two we begin, because in our view both parts are purely coordinate. The one is just as necessary as the other. We must, therefore, decide on the basis of some special reason. Let us pose the following question to our distinctive sphere, which focuses strictly upon Christian ethics: At what point can we begin to use Christian ethics? If we want to give a rigorous answer in the didactical form of theology, we must say that it begins with the rebirth. Which type of behavior begins there? All three. As soon as we consider the rebirth as an accomplished fact in someone, then the power to act is also in him and that means the power to act in all three ways. However, if we ask, what is, strictly speaking, the first thing for which we can assume a certain fitness or from which we can recognize the first thing necessary, each of these answers would be a reason to give priority to one, but it could easily be different. If we now say that in order for the person to manifest the Christian principle, there must already exist in his life's functions an appropriation of that principle, then we already presuppose an activity, and it appears as if we must presuppose the temporal priority of the efficacious behavior.

However, if we ask about what is necessary in the first place, then there is a major contradiction between one's old life and the new life that is just beginning, and this must be properly emphasized, and that happens through the efficacious behavior and, more precisely, through the corrective behavior. Therefore, it seems best to begin with this.